Kentucky Spirits Undistilled

Stories of the Bluegrass State's Famous Haunted Locations

Lisa Westmoreland-Doherty

Schiffer Publishing Ltd

4880 Lower Valley Road, Atglen, Pennsylvania 19310

Disclaimer: Please be aware that many places are open to the public and welcome ghost hunters and thrill seekers alike. However, Eastern Garden Cemetery has many places that are marked "Keep Out" and this is for the safety and protection of both the establishment and public. It is not advised that anyone trespass onto locations that are marked "No Tresspassing."

Other Schiffer Books by Lisa Westmoreland-Doherty:
Louisville Architectural Tours: 19th Century Gems, 0-7643-3038-4, $14.99

Other Schiffer Books on Related Subjects:
A Kentucky Primer: Postcards of Louisville, 0-7643-2570-1, $24.95
Chicago Ghosts, 978-0-7643-2742-1, $14.95

Schiffer Books are available at special discounts for bulk purchases for sales promotions or premiums. Special editions, including personalized covers, corporate imprints, and excerpts can be created in large quantities for special needs. For more information contact the publisher:

Published by Schiffer Publishing Ltd.
4880 Lower Valley Road
Atglen, PA 19310
Phone: (610) 593-1777; Fax: (610) 593-2002
E-mail: Info@schifferbooks.com

For the largest selection of fine reference books on this and related subjects, please visit our web site at: **www.schifferbooks.com.** We are always looking for people to write books on new and related subjects. If you have an idea for a book please contact us at the above address.

This book may be purchased from the publisher. Include $5.00 for shipping. Please try your bookstore first. You may write for a free catalog.

In Europe, Schiffer books are distributed by
Bushwood Books
6 Marksbury Ave.
Kew Gardens
Surrey TW9 4JF England
Phone: 44 (0) 20 8392-8585; Fax: 44 (0) 20 8392-9876
E-mail: info@bushwoodbooks.co.uk
Website: www.bushwoodbooks.co.uk
Free postage in the U.K., Europe; air mail at cost.

Designed by Stephanie Daugherty
Type set in A Charming Font Superexpanded/Cataneo Lt BT/NewsGoth BT

SBN: 978-0-7643-3142-8
Printed in United States of America

Contents

Introduction

There is a terror that stalks us in our dreams, that wakes us in the darkness when we linger in between the states of lucid dreaming and stark reality. There is a fear that lurks in the dreaminess, the place where existence is murky and you're afraid to open your eyes for fear of what you will see. It's what lurks inside us, what we subconsciously fear. Do we fear it because it is unknown, or are we horrified that somewhere deep in the recesses of our consciousness we know that the impossible is often very, very possible? Are our fears the culmination of centuries of stories that we know must have originated somewhere? After all, even the most horrifying and incredible of old wive tales must have had at least a grain of truth in them to begin with. Perhaps, knowing that there is an entire realm of unknown origins and specters is what holds us hostage in the night, sheets pulled tightly around our faces and our eyes squeezed shut, lest we come face to face with the dark figure we can feel watching us, hovering around us, at the foot of the bed. What we cannot explain away, we fear. While many people believe in intangible realms, such as heaven or hell, we are oh-so reluctant to admit that there might be entities and plains of consciousness that fill the gaps and spaces in our belief systems. It is within these realms, or the realm of possibility that our stories begin…and continue.

From the dawn of history mankind has told blood-chilling stories of what lies in the darkness. I remember tales murmured at family events of the "thing" Uncle Bill saw in the woods, or what happened when Granny died become the stories that children love to hear at family reunions and beg to be re-told time after time. I remember listening intently, knowing the whole time that I was not supposed to be anywhere near where the adults were talking. Not often would my uncle be coaxed into telling the story of the *thing* he saw in the woods that night when he and his friend went hunting. Both men were reticent to speak of the incident, usually; but, if you asked either of them to re-tell what happened that dark night, both stories were exactly the same. *Every* detail... *every* description of what they saw and heard matched the story of the other one, which only leads me to believe that what they said happened, DID happen.

It's amazing how the stories of our childhood, the whispered nighttime tales can affect us as adults. Sometimes, when odd things happen, our memories hearken back to the days of innocence when we were told, "Don't be silly. There's no such things as ghosts." We long to believe the ones who told us, even as we recall their own stories and happenings.

As a child, the most beloved story-telling figure was my Uncle, Bill Cravens. He knew so much, had done so many things, and had stories that could curl your six-year-old toes and keep them that way for a month. He often worked nights and this gave him plenty of opportunity to come face-to-face with things that only go bump during those wee hours. Even though the adults took every precaution to make sure my – and my cousins – little ears were far away from any discussion of the afterworld or things in between, we would always find a way to sneak around the corner and crouch down, unseen. We would sit silently, trying to control our breathing so that we could catch every word he was saying. In addition to strange looking bi-pedal humanoid entities that he saw ushering young ones across an abandoned stretch of highway, he was also no stranger to entities that cannot be explained with the word and phrases that we use today. Not often would my uncle be coaxed into telling those stories, but when he was, I could assure you that I would find a way to listen. Of all the members of my family, my Uncle Bill never lied. He was the only one you could trust every time to tell you the truth, even if it meant the truth would scare the bejezzus out of you in the process. That was why we were often sent out from where the grown-ups were talking.

But, on the occasions where several cups of coffee, a few cigarettes, and some good belly laughs with the rest of the family had loosened his tongue, he would become ominously serious and begin to re-tell the story of what he *SAW* that night in the woods. Those were the occasions I lived for, as it gave me the chance to think about the fact there may be things out there that cannot be explained — things that are too frightening to think about and must be reserved for "special" occasions. There may be "things" that roam, hunt, or look for the unsuspecting person who wanders in, even quite accidentally, to their territory.

No stranger to hard work, Uncle Bill used to trap and hunt all through the woods of Shelby County, Kentucky. While it was nasty work, to be certain, he never complained, but tracked through the woods and along the creek banks even in sub-zero temperatures. It was on a crisp autumn night that his most intriguing story occurred. Taking into account that my uncle had at least ten good stories about the strange and paranormal universe that exists beyond us all, I have to say that this one was always my favorite because it happened in the woods behind my childhood home, which made it even more real to me. We had a round table in the kitchen of our home on Bayly Avenue. My uncle would sit back, light a cigarette, and exhale the smoke into the air. At the time I remember thinking that it looked like a ghost swirling around the light fixture above. His face was lined and serious as he began the story.

"It was about three o'clock in the morning," he would begin. "Mike and I had been out coon hunting and hadn't had much luck. We walked up and down Floyd's Fork for the better part of the night and hadn't had much luck. You know you can't coon hunt in the daytime because they're night animals and only come out in the small hours of the morning. Anyway, we had gotten a little worried because two of the dogs took off and hadn't come back yet. We worried because it is known that a coon will drown a dog if it has the chance. So, we were walking around, looking for the dogs, when all of a sudden we heard something behind us. It was an overcast night, but we could make out some sort of shape that was standing there, looking at us. It was about one hundred feet away, but we could tell that it was watching us because it had eyes unlike anything we had ever seen before. They were red and they were glowing..."

Now it was usually right about there that adults who were hearing the story for the first time would stop and laugh nervously, asking my uncle what he had been smoking that night. And, he, patiently, would do one of two things: he would adamantly declare that was not the case, or, he would stop his story in the middle and not go one word further because his integrity had been insulted. It all depended on his mood and the people he was with at the time. Sometimes, he wouldn't even tell the story at all. But, most of the time it was just us—his family—and he would indulge us a little and continue.

Later, we my family and I moved out to the country we lived right down the road from Uncle Bill and his family. What is interesting is that the body of water where they saw the creature runs for a couple of miles is called Floyd's Fork. Our home sat right on Floyd's Fork. Now, the fact that our home sat right on the creek where my Uncle saw the creature is not really that strange. What is unusual is that we were never sure when our dogs or animals would suddenly disappear. While it must be taken into consideration that foxes and coyotes do live in the area, as well as possums and other carnivorous animals, they usually only attack small animals such as chickens or other poultry. My mother finally gave up on trying to raise chickens because of the disappearances. A fox or other animal would have certainly left evidence behind, such as feathers, blood, or signs of a struggle. When one – or ten – would disappear, there would be nothing left behind. Additionally, there were three dogs that disappeared, as well. They would run off into the woods, as hunting dogs do, and never return. We always hoped that they were kidnapped, or dognapped, by hunters who wanted good dogs. While that was a sad and painful thing to imagine, it was so much worse to think about them becoming a snack for that thing my uncle saw...

"Now, Mike and I trapped all through those woods from the time we were kids and we knew every animal look and sound that was back there. And, we knew that this was nothing like anything we had ever seen before in our life. We would walk a few feet and stop, looking over our shoulders. We could see the eyes—nothing more—and could tell it was keeping up with us, stalking us. Now, we weren't ones who were looking to confront something we didn't know anything about in a place that was far away from anything and anyone. And, you don't go shootin' at something when you don't know what it is. So, we picked up the pace a little...and so did it. We climbed over a barbed wire fence (pronounced in Kentucky parlance as 'Bob Wire') and started to run. I swear to you that thing either jumped the fence or was so tall that it stepped right over it. It was keepin' up with us and we were starting to get real scared about what it would do when — and if — it caught up with us. We got so far that we could see the truck from where we were and all we had to do was clear the creek and we'd be back to the road. We jumped the creek with all our might and made for the truck. I turned back around to see if it was still following us and then we stopped. The thing on the other side had stopped on the opposite side of the creek. We stood there and watched it, watching us. Then, it reared back its head and let out the most blood-curdling scream I have ever heard in my life. It sounded like a woman getting her head cut off. Then it turned and made its way back into the woods. Mike and I jumped into the car and took off. We came back for the dogs later — in the daytime."

That story always made my blood run cold — and still does to this day. I know as I sit here that my uncle is not a liar, nor even a stretcher of the truth. He prides himself on his logic and not giving in to those thoughts that would take him into the realm of the unbelievable. That, along with the fact that he was usually so reticent to speak of the incident makes it all the more credible with me. It's odd how family events will often turn one's thoughts to the likelihood of things existing outside the realm of belief. While I, myself, had not experienced anything out of the ordinary, I could very well believe that there were others out there who had. Now, my parents on the other hand, told very different, but just as believable stories about their own experiences with death and ghosts. It is as real to them when they tell about my paternal grandfather's death today as it was in 1972, when it happened.

My grandfather was Louis Carter Westmoreland—I have no definitive memory of him at all. I was not yet two when he died, but somewhere lodged in my memory is the vivid recollection of his false teeth scaring me to death, and yet being oddly fascinated by them and trying to take them out of his mouth. I can't say whether I remember it first hand or if I remember being told about it, but it seems very real to me. I was a favorite of his, according to my mother, who tells me about how he took me when I was just a babe in his arms and carried me into his bedroom. There, he put his own solid gold baby ring on my finger and carried me around with it on my own fat little baby finger. My mother tells me that he loved me dearly because I so looked like the Westmoreland babies and had such a sunny disposition. Whatever the reason, I still have the ring to this day and feel connected to him even though I never really knew him.

It was the spring of 1972. My grandparents loved to go to Nolin Lake where they would fish and relax, like most retired people like to do. Pawpaw, as we called him, had gone to the doctor to be checked out before leaving for the lake. Having heart problems made him conscious of the need to check in with someone and get their approval before starting out of town anywhere. Worried that he might run into trouble in a place where the nearest hospital is miles away, he believed he was doing the smart and responsible thing. However, what life teaches us is that when we have a date with Death, he will not be stood up nor put off until another time — no matter what precautions we take to the contrary. The doctor checked him and pronounced him fit to go. So he and my grandmother, Maudie, set out for the lake and a nice, relaxing time. They arrived there together and she began to unpack their things and change the sheets on the bed, since the cabin had not been used yet that season. Papaw, however, couldn't wait to get to the lake to fish. He decided to go out first and go fishing while she took care of the household things. He never made it. According to the men who were driving behind him, he began to swerve in his car. Thinking he was drunk, they followed closely behind him and watched as his car veered off the road and went into a cornfield. They ran to see what was going on and found him, dead. They said that he was already gone when they arrived on the scene because he was gurgling in the back of his throat, often known locally as the "death rattle." The death certificate officially read that the time of death was 5:50 p.m. I am sure that he died before that, but, officially, that was the pronouncement. My mother, whose mind is like a steel trap when it comes to remembering the history and stories of the family, tells the story and the happenings after like this:

> They took him to the hospital and pronounced him dead on arrival. They had no way of contacting Mamaw because his driver's license was his only identification and no one knew that he was there with someone else. The license gave his address as Louisville and so they sent someone to their home to let them know what happened. Of course, no one was home. We lived one street over from them and it just so happened that we were driving by to check on things

since we knew they were out of town. The police were there when we went by and they told us what happened. We all broke down and cried, because it was so sudden and he had just been to the doctor that morning. The body was at Rogers Funeral Home and arrangements would have to be made to bring it to Louisville, but the worst part was that no one had told Mamaw what had happened. She was still at the camp by the lake, waiting for him to come home. My father decided to drive down by himself and get her. It was early in the morning when my father finally got there and she was beside herself with worry, not knowing where her husband was. When she heard the news, she reacted as everyone who hears of an unexpected death reacts, with immense sorrow and disbelief. It was a terrible time for the family. Their house, still locked up from when they left it just hours before, was empty. It was decided that we would go home, gather a few things, and then go to their house for the night so that she wouldn't be alone. We all met at her house first and then went to ours to get clothes and necessities. It was dark and sad. The living room sat to the right of the entry hall and when everyone came in and turned on the light, they stopped in their tracks. The huge sunburst clock that had been wildly popular in the 1970s had stopped working. It had stopped at 5:50 exactly. Even odder than that was the fact that it was oozing something thick and strange from the back of the clock. It was not battery acid, nor anything that my parents could identify. In fact, the inner workings of the clock were clean! Whatever it was soaked into the wallpaper and from that day forward, no matter how many times my parents papered over it, it would always find a way to seep back through. Months and years later, they even cleaned the area and covered it over before papering it again. It still found a way to come through. My brother and sister went upstairs to their attic room to get their clothes. The light refused to work. It wouldn't turn on. Then, when they turned it off, it came back on. Frightened, they all piled in the car and made their way to my grandmother's house. Before they could even get in the door, my grandmother was walking the floor, in a terrible state of confusion and grief. She took them over to the clock on the television and showed them what she found when she came in. The television sat catty-corner and had the clock sitting on top of it. They were both plugged into the socket behind the TV and you would have had to pull the TV out to get to the plug, a feat that a one-armed woman in her sixties would have had great difficulty doing in the best of circumstances. But, the oddity that had startled her so badly was that not only had the clock stopped at, yes, you guessed it, 5:50, but the plug had been pulled out of the socket. The TV, however, remained plugged in correctly. There were many other incidences associated with Papaw's death, but I was too young to remember them. I do believe my family when they tell the stories because it upsets them to this day. The one thing my mother always says is that when people die, check the electrical or battery operated appliances in the house. For some strange reason, when something is trying to get your attention, it will often manifest in those kinds of areas.

The point to this all is that most of us have had run-ins with things we cannot explain. We see things out of the corners of our eyes and then turn, only to find they are gone. We hear things in the night and dismiss them as the settling of the house or branches against the house. We smell fragrances of perfume or, in my grandfather's case, we smell the scent of his favorite pipe even though there is no possible explanation other than perhaps sensory memory. Somewhere, deep inside us all, there is the hope that those we love have not gone far away from us and we look for evidence of this wherever we can find it so that we will reconcile within ourselves the fact that life does not end when our hearts cease to beat. The stories that go along with this hope are what sustain us and, yes, scare us a little. So, for all those skeptics, like me, who hope that one day they will find enough evidence to prove that life doesn't end at the end of a last breath, I hope the tales included within will both entertain you and give you pause to ponder the possibility of an existence beyond this life.

1

Haunted Historical Bardstown

Old Talbott Tavern

Question: How many ghosts does it take to scare the pants off a skeptical writer? Answer: None. I was scared before I even approached Historic Bardstown just because of the reputation it has as a haven for supernatural and otherworldly entities. Bardstown has given safe passage and refuge to famous — and infamous — figures and many argue that they must have liked it so well that they decided to stay, even after death. Figures such as exiled King of France, Louis Phillipe, and his entourage; Abraham Lincoln and his family; Stephen Foster; and Jesse James all found a refuge in the Talbott Tavern—and some liked it so well they continue to visit and roam the familiar halls of the restaurant/bed and breakfast, frightening visitors and reminding the workers that they are still here, milling around, though time may have forgotten them. As with most "haunted" places, this writer was highly skeptical as to whether or not the stories were true, but had such an ominous feeling inside that I knew something would happen on the night I went to visit — I just was not sure what it would be or what I would see. As I am not a ghost chaser or investigator of the paranormal, I felt that if I did see or report anything strange from this small town and its dwellings, it would be a little more credible than if I were a full blown believer in aliens, UFOs, and shadow people. What I can say about the Talbott Tavern is that I will tell the entire story as

Historic Talbott Tavern from the outside.

it was told to me, include my feelings and report what happened on the night I went there, show you the pictures, and let **YOU** decide for yourself. I will say in advance that I cannot logically explain what I have on my pictures. I can honestly say that all the pictures were taken with the same camera, a Nikon D 100, and when I took the pictures, I could see nothing with my naked eye. Out of five hundred digital pictures that were taken that night, fifteen came back with what I would label "anomalies" on them—*strange things that I cannot explain and cannot tell you how or what they are.* I will tell you what some experts in the field have told me, but again, I leave it to you, the reader, to draw your own conclusions.

Most locals and those from Kentucky who pass by Bardstown on their way to visit Federal Hill, also known as My Old Kentucky Home, are familiar with Talbott Tavern and its scrumptious cuisine. They go for an overnight visit to stay in one of the oldest jails in Kentucky, currently made into a bed and breakfast, or at the Tavern itself. Many of the local and out-of-town tourists never catch wind of the fact that they might just have to share their overnight accommodations with a specter or two — if they are lucky. The night I went to visit the Talbott Tavern, my memory hearkened back to the days of my own childhood, when my parents took me to Bardstown to see the "Stephen Foster Story." I was about nine or ten years old, a great age to appreciate the gorgeous antebellum costumes and the ambiance of an outdoor theatre. The last time my parents had taken me to an outdoor theatre was when I was three, which should say something about the experience itself. It had nothing to do with the performance and everything to do

Talbott Tavern Interior. Notice the orb in the corner.

Talbott Tavern Interior — Huge orb in above the chair. This room is notorious for spirit activity, according to Patti Starr. There is a little girl who loves to open the doors and will often do it on command.

with how I reacted to it. We attempted to see the "Daniel Boone Story," another riveting outdoor adventure that told of the settling of the land in Kentucky and the events surrounding the exploration of the land around the area of Boonesboro. For the most part all went well until the Native Americans captured and killed Boone's little boy. I had no idea at the time that this was theater and was certain that I was witness to a horrible atrocity. I began to scream and cry inconsolably, forcing my mother to remove me from the amphitheatre. Even though the years passed and I grew older and more mature, my parents waited quite awhile before taking me to the theatre again.

Even though twenty-five or thirty years have passed, I can still tell you what I ordered the night my parents took me to Talbott Tavern for dinner. Excited about the performance, the elaborate costumes, and singing, I had no idea what to order. I ordered a Hot Brown, which is a regional favorite. Named after the Brown Hotel in Louisville, it is a gorgeous creation of turkey breast on toast, with tomato slices. The concoction is covered with cheese or Mornay sauce, depending on how strictly one adheres to the traditional recipe. It is then put into the oven to bake and only removed when the cheese is bubbly brown. It is then topped with two or three strips of bacon and served hot. I can still remember how good that Hot Brown tasted and on the night I went to investigate the Talbott Tavern, I made sure I ordered the same exact dish so that I could see if it had changed after all these years. I am pleased to report that the food was still as delicious as I remembered. Tasting that dish was like savoring a precious moment of my childhood and I held it as long as I could before swallowing.

The History

The Talbott Tavern has a long, rich history, so it's not surprising that many claim to have seen apparitions and been visited by a ghostly poke in the ribs by a fun-loving figure who

Talbott Tavern Interior. God only knows what this is. This picture was shot into a pitch black hallway. There were no lights anywhere. I would personally love to know what this is!

apparently likes to startle curious guests. The Tavern itself it an extremely old building and is reported to be the oldest western stagecoach stop in America. Built in 1779, the rough stone exterior speaks of longevity and fortitude, two traits that exemplify the American spirit both then — and today. Renowned for its traditional Southern hospitality and cuisine, as well as its Bourbon Bar and extensive Bourbon selection, the Talbott Tavern boasts five rooms where travelers can experience the warmth and graciousness of the Tavern's hosts. It is within these rooms that those who have stayed there overnight or passed through as visitors have reported many strange and unexplained events. Talbott Tavern plays host to those who come to visit for its history, as well as those who seek a more supernatural experience.

It was in my search for "haunted locations" that I happened upon the Tavern and began my exploration into the stories that surround it. In addition to being one of the hottest nightspots in Bardstown and the surrounding area, it boasts a selection of fine Kentucky Bourbon that is second to none, hands down. From the time it was established in 1779, the Tavern ran non-stop as an area of respite for road-weary travelers and local patrons. However, on March 7, 1998, the Tavern suffered extensive damage in a fire that destroyed many parts of the original structure. Rooms that kings and dignitaries had slept in, previously available to the public, were now damaged to the extent that renovations and re-structuring had to be done before it could safely be re-opened. Fortunately for the Tavern, Jim Beam Distilleries recognized the importance of this historic landmark and donated wood for the hardwood floors so that the Tavern could be rebuilt in the same style that it had been originally. It re-opened for business in November of 1999 and one might think that the story stops there, as does the ghost tales and legends. According to Patti Starr, local ghost hunter and historical expert, the fire did not diminish any of the paranormal activity in the Tavern.

Talbott Tavern Exterior — The "Jesse James" window. Often guests will capture him staring out of this window, still wearing his trademark duster and hat.

The Legend of Jesse James and the Talbott Tavern

It's no secret that notorious outlaw Jesse James robbed the Russellville, Kentucky Bank owned by Nimrod and Co. on March 20, 1868. It's well known legend and lore that he once hid out in Mammoth Cave in order to avoid capture and then sneaked out of a small, secret passage. What is not often talked about, however, are his familial ties to Bardstown and possible reasons that he still walks the halls of the Talbott Tavern yet today, pulling the hair of the patrons or emerging just in time to scare the wits out of the unsuspecting lodger. Jesse James's mother was no stranger to the area and neither was he. Born in Midway Kentucky, his mother, Zerelda Cole, attended St. Catherine's College, earning a degree, which was highly unusual for women in that day and age. Described as strong-willed and having a keen intellect, it would appear that she loved all **three** of her husbands and all **eight** of her children!

This gave her two most notorious sons, Frank and Jesse, lots of relatives and points of contact during their crime spree. There were always people willing to help them, even if it was breaking the law. One story associated with the Tavern is that Donnie Pence, a cousin of Frank and Jesse, was the sheriff in town. He was staying next door at the Old Jailor's Inn when he caught wind that the US Marshals were getting close to Bardstown. Jesse was staying at the Tavern and Donnie sent word that he needed to get out of town immediately. As legend tells it, unbeknownst to the marshal, there is an underground tunnel that runs underneath the Tavern and comes out on the other side of the courthouse. Horses were always waiting on the other side — just in case the boys needed to get away fast. As luck would have it, Donnie got the word to him just in time. The marshal showed up only to find that Jesse was nowhere in sight and, according to the locals, had not been there at all! The question might be raised as to why the locals would protect such a notorious criminal? The answer, as told to me, was simple. They *loved* him! It was not uncommon for Jesse to stay with a local family or go visiting, get drunk, and stay the night. The legend says that the people adored Jesse because "he never hurt anyone and he was a big tipper! If he stayed at your house to have dinner, he would leave a gold coin underneath his plate."

The people of Bardstown must have found it very difficult to despise someone who practiced such generosity when times were so hard. It cannot be denied that as much as Jesse loved to socialize, he also loved to drink. His connection to the Tavern does not end with his escape through the underground tunnel. He came back several times before his ultimate demise and was fond of getting drunk and going upstairs to one of the bedrooms to sleep it off. On one occasion, he slept in the room that King Louis Phillipe of France had once slept in *and* practiced his artistry on the wall. Louis had painted a mural of a forest and birds flying overhead, a rather pastoral scene, perhaps to create an idyllic retreat from all the post-Revolution nastiness he escaped. Jesse was in that room, extremely intoxicated, when he heard a noise. He awoke, not knowing where he was, but saw birds flying all around him! He pulled out his gun and shot at them, not realizing he was actually shooting at King Louis's mural! Even though the fire did great damage to what is now known as the Jesse James room, the mural still exists, as do the bullet holes in the walls where the birds are painted.

Jesse James is a prominent spirit in the Tavern according to the workers—and according to Patti Starr, a local ghost hunter and paranormal expert. She heads the walking ghost tour of Bardstown and is extremely knowledgeable in both the history of the place and its paranormal activity. She is fond of retelling the stories and has had many personal run-ins with the spirits themselves, especially that of Jesse James. "He thinks it's funny to startle people," she said about him. He is almost always seen as a solid figure and is usually wearing a duster. It is common for people to be walking in the hall and feel a sharp poke. This is almost always attributed to James. At one time, the Tavern hosted a "Mystery Dinner Theatre" where the diners were able to participate in the actual drama that was presented. During one such performance, the scene called for a séance. The actors were performing and calling on the spirits, but no one was prepared for it to actually work! As they acted the scene, the "fake" séance brought Jesse right out of the shadows and in front of the actors and all the diners! According to Patti Starr, Jesse is often photographed in the windows on the second floor of the Tavern and simply likes to show up in the hallways to startle unsuspecting guests.

The Old Stockade welcomes you to the Jailor's Inn and reminds you of what it was like to be punished in the old days!

The Old Jailer's Inn

Nothing beckons the hunters of the paranormal like places where people die tragically or suddenly — even if that place is a foundation of social justice. I have often wondered what tales the death chamber of a prison holds inside it, which is, I know, a sick and twisted mental consideration, but fascinating to ponder nonetheless. Those who die to pay for their crimes are usually as unwilling to go gently into that good night as

Exterior of the Old Jailor's Inn

were their victims. When you see the Jailer's Inn, it is hard to believe that so welcoming a bed and breakfast was once the bastion of justice for this small Kentucky town. The criminals would be held inside and, often, it would be the last place where they stayed, as the gallows were erected outside in the back courtyard. A high rock wall surrounds the courtyard and the large, wooden gates at the rear leave just enough space that a person would be able to get an excellent view of the last moments of a condemned man's life. I can only imagine how many people scaled the fifteen- or twenty-foot wall to get a better view. From the front, however, the lovely white building would give no indication that this was a working jail from 1819 to 1987, except perhaps for the large stockade located in the front yard. Put there as more of a themed focal point, it reminds visitors that this was not a nice place to spend your time in the early days. While not original to the building, it is an excellent antique and could probably tell many stories of the people who spent time locked up in it.

The History

Built in 1819, the Jailer's Inn functioned as the county seat of Nelson County and housed all of its criminals. The jailor would live on the first floor of the building and the inmates on the second. According to legend, the first room to the right on the second floor is the most haunted. It still has the original hand-hewn boards with the original shackles still attached to them. The story is told that a man was staying in that room, which is now a fully functioning guest room in the bed and breakfast. There had been a salesman who would frequently stop and make this his room of choice each time. However, during his stay one evening, he noticed that there was another man in his room. Startled, he turned around to see who was there and the man simply...walked past him and *through* the wall! Interestingly, the wall that he walked through used to be an archway where the door used to be! Could it be that the spirit this man encountered was simply walking in death as he had in life, remembering the establishment only as it used

I took several pictures of the windows and the outside reflective surfaces because Patti Starr said it was very common for people to capture "faces in the windows."

This is another "you be the judge" picture. I thought I could make out the outline of a female in the lower pane, but others who have looked at these pictures say that they see several people in it, depending on how you look at it.

to be? There are so many stories of the haunting of this old jail and I was pleased to find an actual newspaper article from May 28, 1909 that speaks directly to it. It read as follows:

The Nelson Co. jail is haunted. It was erected in 1874 and a number of gruesome occurrences have occurred within its walls. George MURRELL, the notorious outlaw, after being fatally shot by Marshal HUNTER, lingered and died in the most awful agony. Harvey PASH, a Negro murderer, and Phil EVANS, a Negro rapist, spent their last months upon earth within the gloomy edifice and were finally led forth to die upon the scaffold which still stands, a forbidding looking object, close to the walls of the building.

Martin HILL, a wife murderer, died in a cell of the jail of a consuming fever, after weeks of lingering torture, and thereby cheated the gallows. It is said by those in a position to know that it is the spirit of this last named who haunts the jail, and surely his crime was horrible enough and his death of such agony as to cause his miserable spirit to know no rest.

Detail of window.

In the early part of 1885, Martin Hill walked into a neighbor's house, where his wife had fled to escape his brutal treatment, and shot the defenseless woman down without a word of warning. Hill's reputation had always been unsavory, and though he came from a good family, his career had been thoroughly wicked. His last crowning criminal act, the inhuman murder of his wife, aroused the deepest indignation and the women of his neighborhood swore that if he was not hanged they would themselves tear down the courthouse stone by stone. However, before he could be brought to final trial, he was smitten by fever, which resulted in his death. Citizens who attended him in his last illness avow that his sufferings were the most terrible ever witnessed, and that during his moments of delirium his ravings and blasphemies were awful to hear.

Prisoners have since been confined in the jail hear strange sounds in the cell where he died. He is heard, it is alleged, pacing up and down, as was his wont, during his confinement. He is also heard to groan and toss restlessly upon his bunk, and as a climax to the whole, the blood-curdling scream he omitted while struggling in the throes of death, rings through the stone corridors with thrilling distinctness. These and many other manifestations are spoken of, and he is considered a brave man indeed, who willingly ventures near the haunted cell after night.

Within a few yards of the haunted structure is situated the original old stone prison, built near the close of the last century by "Old Stone Hammer" METCALFE, afterwards Governor of Kentucky. John FITCH, the inventor of the steamboat, died in the old jail. He was not a prisoner, however, but was boarding with the jailer, Alexander McCOWEN, who was his friend. Many noted criminals have looked through the bars of this old prison house, among them WATSON, the murderer of two men, who was the first white man legally executed in Nelson Co. Three Negro slaves, who assassinated their master, James G. MAXWELL and Samuels H. CALHOUN, a Federal soldier, who murdered Wm. SUTHERLAND, a prominent citizen, were led to the gallows from this old jail. (*Bardstown Standard*) [8]

These reports of strange sounds and apparitions are not occasional occurrences and many visit the Jailer's Inn for exactly that reason. While there may not be a visitation of spirits every single day, there are enough people who report strange happenings to make this an interesting stop on your visit to Bardstown. Also, since it is in such close proximity to the Talbott Tavern, one could theoretically make this a two-for-one haunted stop! Have dinner with Jesse James or one of the many spirits who linger in the Tavern and then head over to the Jailer's Inn to see if you can hear anything go bump in the night!

The Chapeze House

In a city as old as Bardstown, it's not unusual to have two or three haunted locations within walking distance of each other. People used to have to walk or ride horses when they wanted to go visiting or do business in the city, so the buildings were meant to be convenient for the local patrons. For instance, with the Talbott Tavern, it amuses me to think that the local drunks would go over, get their bellies full, create a disturbance, and would then be conveniently escorted just yards away to the jail, sleeping off their inebriation in a nice, cozy drunk tank. The Chapeze House is located just down the street from both establishments and is the third location on the local ghost trek led by Patti Starr; it's supposedly haunted by a nameless, faceless woman who continues to walk in shame along its historical hallways.

The History

One of the added bonuses of writing a book about haunted places is listening to the many tales and legends that accompany the place itself. Reporting those stories as fact, however, I have great difficulty with and therefore do an immense amount of research to find out if there is any truthful basis for the story. Sometimes I find evidence that supports the story and other times, it will refute what people have believed for decades, if not hundreds of years. The Chapeze House, however, has a story that supports what the locals have told me and I have actually found evidence to reinforce the local lore.

When our country was still in its infancy and General George Washington was beginning to prepare for war with Great Britain, the Marquis de LaFayette was preparing in France to come to the assistance of the fledgling nation that would dare rebel against the nation who had defeated the Spanish Armada in 1588 and had not let the rest of the world forget it since. Long time rivals,

Exterior of the Chapeze House windows.

France and Britain had learned to co-exist, but France supported any country that threatened to give England a black eye. It was more out of spite than a true desire to see America succeed that France began sending reinforcements to help us in our endeavor. During this time, LaFayette came to America with fourteen French army officers, one of whom was Dr. Henri Chapeze, a surgeon. When they arrived, the year was 1777 and America was in the throes of war. Chapeze served under General Washington in the Continental Army. After that war was over, Chapeze married Sarah Kenny, who had come here from Ireland. Very little is known or written about Sarah, but I feel certain that she is at the heart of the scandal and the subsequent disintegration of the original Chapeze family. According to the legend, Dr. Chapeze came home one day to find his wife in the arms of another man. The adultery, especially in such a small town, was unbearable, as was finding his wife in such a compromising position. According to legend, she lived in shame until her death and then Dr. Chapeze died in 1810, leaving the house to his son, Benjamin. As I said, that

Patti Starr in front of Chapeze House. Often, people will show up in the windows behind her and Henri is usually one of them!

was the story as it was told to me. Short and sweet, but to the point. However, the mystery only begins with Dr. Henri (Henry) Chapeze and his unfaithful wife, but it does not end in 1810 with his death because according to records I have uncovered, when Henry Chapeze left Kentucky, it was to start a new life somewhere else.

There is probably some modicum of truth to the story of the adultery, but I wondered how I would substantiate that claim. If the stories of the haunting and what precipitated it are true, then how would I ever find the necessary documents to prove it? The Internet has proven to be a faithful and more than useful resource. Even in the early 1900s people were allowed to divorce their spouses, though it was still frowned upon. Marriage was supposed to be forever, as was fidelity — at least on the part of the female. However, the rumors of adultery must be true because in 1803, Henry (Henri) divorced Sarah. Noted in *Littells Laws of Kentucky, Volume 3*, the following was recorded:

"An act concerning the marriage of HENRY CHAPEZE approved Dec. 1, 1803. This act (sic) authorised him to sue in the Nelson circuit court, for a divorce from his wife, SARAH CHAPEZE, and to obtain it on a jury's finding that she had deserted him, intermarried with another man, and was, and for a long time, had been of loose and incontinent habits."[9]

Henry had enough by 1803 and Sarah sank into oblivion and despair, literally "losing face" with all members of society. They were a well-respected family and to bring such shame upon the name of Chapeze must have been unbearable to Henry. According to legend, Nelson County records, and oral history Henry died around 1810. Here is where the discrepancy arises. According to my findings, Henry did not die, even though his will was probated in 1813. It appears that he left Kentucky, his son, and all the bad memories behind him to start another life in Piqua, Ohio. It was there that he married Elizabeth Morrow Chapeze and had at least two children, Henrietta and Rosetta. We know from records in Piqua that he set up a medical practice there in 1813 — the same year his will was probated in Nelson County, Kentucky! Records read that:

"One of the earliest physicians in Miami County was Dr. Henry Chapeze, who came to Ohio in 1814 from his former home in Kentucky. He built a brick office on the corner of Wayne and Water streets in Piqua. In 1820 Dr. John O'Ferrall joined him and they worked hard to take care of the sick in the community. Other doctors in the early history of Piqua are: Drs. Jackson, Teller, Jorden, Hendershott, and Worrall."[10]

Another, more detailed, item follows:

"About the close of the War of 1812, Henry Chapeze, of Kentucky, a well educated physician, located at Piqua. His office and residence were on the southwest corner of Wayne and Water Streets, on the lot now occupied by the house of Hiram Brooks, Esq. A brick office erected on this lot was the first building of that material in the village limits, and is well remembered today by many of the older inhabitants. Dr. John O'Ferrall settled in Piqua about 1820, and these two gentlemen have the honor of being the pioneer physicians of the town and of the northern part of the county. Both continued in the practice of their profession for many years, riding over large extents of forest country, sometimes without roads, at other times over ways almost impassable, where the worst mud holes and deepest marshes were bridged over by rows of round logs, making no very secure causeway for either horses or man. The rude cabin and rough fare of the early settlers were their resting-place and their refreshment; a scanty renumeration, and very frequently none at all, was the reward rendered for services; but these faithful men toiled on, waited and hoped for better days, and lived to see at least their dawn if not their full development. Dr. Chapeze died about 1828; but O'Ferrall, a younger and more vigorous man, survived until 1850, living to see the country which he entered as a wilderness blooming with improvements and filled with elements of wealth and progress."[11]

Dr. Chapeze died in 1828? How could this possibly be? Sometimes the heartbreak and shame of a shattered life is more than a person can bear and perhaps this was what happened to Dr. Chapeze. What we do know is that his name and his legacy lived on in the form of his grandson, Henry C. Houston (son of Henrietta and William Houston), who went on to study medicine and help his father in his practice in Piqua, Ohio. Did Benjamin ever know that he had half sisters? The family, as far as I can tell, remained divided as the city of Bardstown still only tells of how Dr. Chapeze died there. It is in the uncovering of family and historical secrets such as these that we find foundation on which the stories of the haunted Chapeze House are built.

The Faceless Lady and the Little Boy

The Chapeze House was the tourism center for quite some time in Bardstown. However, the workers all knew that something strange was going on inside the house and were not quite sure what it was. Televisions would turn off and then on again. Papers would mysteriously fly up into the air, when there was no breeze or fan to blow them. Toilets would flush by themselves. A person would be typing on her computer, get up to get something and come back to find that the font had been changed from large to small. Lights would blink off and on, as if to get someone's attention. Many things have been reported at the Chapeze House and no one has any explanation for them.

Patti Starr explains that a little boy has reportedly been seen sitting outside the house on the front steps. Cameras have captured him and a child's laughter can frequently be heard coming from inside the house. While the workers and locals fondly call him "Ornery Henri," he is often reported as being ill-tempered or a little mean, like a spiteful child. He might pinch you or kick you, according to Starr, who says that it's "like a little kid teasing you."

However, according to the history I now know, I can't imagine that it's the ghost of Henri Chapeze, since he was a grown man when he began building the home. It could be the spirit of Benjamin, the little boy who had to live with his mother's shame and the abandonment of his father. These two things would put any child in a state of emotional shock and having to live with his mother's betrayal of his father every single day – and having to become the "man of the house" at an early age – might have had an impact that has lasted beyond the grave. Even though Benjamin grew up to be a fine upstanding citizen of Bardstown and continued the family line down into the present day, perhaps the trauma of what he saw and suffered as a child never left him and the residual effects are what are still witnessed today.

Early one morning one of the workers at the Chapeze House was coming around the back. She noticed that there was a woman with long dark hair standing at the window in what used to be the kitchen area. Alarmed, the worker immediately went in to see who was in the building, even though it had not opened yet. As she approached the figure, she gasped. The dark haired woman turned to face the worker and when she did, the worker realized that where there should have been a set of eyes staring back at her, there was just skin. The woman had no face at all! You can imagine her horror and disgust as she realized that what she was seeing could not be possible and that she was staring at the faceless image of a ghost. The story does not end there, as the "faceless lady" has been captured many times "looking" out of windows and doors. She just stands there until...*disappearing into thin air*. So who is this lady? My guess is that it's Sarah Kenny Chapeze, the woman who "lost face" with her husband, her family, and the entirety of Nelson County society when she had her illicit affair. For a person to symbolically represent shame by having no facial features in the afterlife is something I have never heard, but I do not doubt nor discount that it could be true, however. Many times the choices we make, both good and bad, follow us the rest of our lives and continue to haunt our families long after we are gone. Perhaps it is for that reason the members of the Bardstown community choose to remember that Dr. Chapeze died rather than say he abandoned his son, Benjamin. Sarah Kenny must have suffered in that way, too. Her shame followed her to the grave and must have haunted Benjamin until the end, too. I like to think that if the faceless lady is Sarah, somehow she will find a way to forgive herself and pass into a place of rest. In the end, guilt is sometimes the hardest thing to let go of and continuing to punish ourselves makes it seem as if we are paying penance for whatever petty crime we committed. Letting go of that guilt is what any of us has to do in order to move forward. If only Sarah Kenny were able to do that, even in the afterlife, perhaps she, too could move on from her own self-imposed prison.

2

Haunted Cemeteries

Eastern Cemetery & Crematorium

A cemetery is not an excursion for the faint of heart, no matter what season or time of day it is visited. Usually, most of us try our best to stay away and not think about the fact that somewhere in the world, there is a burial plot or an urn waiting to have our name engraved on it for posterity to remember. I have always felt, perhaps incorrectly and ignorantly so, that cemeteries are the very last places that a spirit would cling to, as the person very likely did not die there or have any close ties to the area itself. I always envisioned cemeteries as a repository for a shell than a place where the dead would linger. Many of the readings and research I have done suggests that spirits like to be where there is life and energy abounding. Some have speculated that this is because just like people, spirits are drawn to those whose energy is fresh and positive. The positive energy acts as a beacon, of sorts. Just as we like to be around those people who shine and glow, making us feel good, so do those who have passed on. Yet, contrary to my beliefs and speculations about where a spirit would be if it existed, my preliminary research indicated that Eastern Cemetery on Bardstown Road was haunted. I had personally never been there, but strange tales of a weeping angel and an infant burial ground behind the crematorium was enough to pique my interest and send me out to take a few pictures and see what, if anything, I could find.

The cemetery itself is run down, but is still a peaceful place to walk on a fall day.

If I need to remind you, my readers, of anything, it is that I began this book with a staunch and firm stance on the subject of ghosts. I do not believe in them. I do, however, believe in investigating all things interesting that just may prove me a liar. It is with this in mind that I tell the story about the picture of Eastern Cemetery Crematorium.

That windy November morning was much warmer than I expected it to be. Sometimes, even though it's probably a sin, I am grateful for global warming, as it renders a heavy jacket or coat unnecessary for much of the year in Kentucky. On this particular day, my usual, albeit unwilling, and just as skeptical partner, my husband, Jim, was not in the mood to go trekking around a cemetery. He wanted to stick around the house and do laundry, a request that I am certainly smart enough *not* to turn down or

An angel looks down from above adding a benevolent feeling to this restless place.

discourage. However, I also know that it's a foolhardy person who goes traipsing around a strange cemetery and crematorium alone. It is not the ghosts that I worried about, but the transients, drug dealers, or the mentally ill homeless people who might have decided to camp out around there the night before. So, with this in mind, I picked up the phone to call a good friend of mine, Joe Guthrie, to see if he might be interested in a little ghost hunting.

Good naturedly, he agreed and I was immediately thankful that Joe was going, as he was often much more courageous than I was in our younger days at the university. If I needed someone to go first into the darkness, I knew that Joe would be that someone and dare anything to show itself. He is just that kind of guy. Fearless.

The morning was crisp, but not bitterly cold, as we made our way around the headstones. Every so often, I would stop and take a picture, shooting into the trees and the distance... just in case SOMETHING decided to show up. I found interesting headstones, one in particular that was English on one side and Asian calligraphy on the other. It was stunningly beautiful. I shot over three hundred pictures in the cemetery, but nothing came back — until we decided to go where we had no business going. The crematorium. The rumors are true, I must confess. There is a statue of an angel and a piece of it is broken off. You are not supposed to touch the broken piece or try to put it back in its place, so the story goes, for fear of disturbing the ones who sleep beneath. The angel is supposed to guard or watch over the plot that is specifically for the infants, back behind the crematorium. I did investigate the stones and there are many infant and child graves in the back. However, it looked more to me like family burial plots, as there were adults there, too. It was not scary until Joe found an entrance into the crematorium. It was pitch black and there was no electricity in any of the rooms below. The door we entered was at the basement and was very likely where the bodies would be taken immediately after they had been released for cremation, as the doors were double doors and the road that led to the doors was large enough for a hearse to back up to, if necessary. Once inside, I felt immediately ill at ease and was quite certain we might be mugged — or worse. There was a large furnace that looked as if it could accommodate two bodies, one on the top and one on the bottom. I took numerous pictures of it, but nothing of any interest to me showed up. Again, it must be remembered that I am not a ghost chaser or investigator. I am a writer and a skeptic, which makes what I have to report

The headless statue stands and there is a story that says it must not be touched or else the person who touches it will incur the wrath of the spirit who inhabits the monument.

so much more interesting, in my own opinion. However, I began shooting my camera into the darkness. Fortunately, my camera is pretty good and I was able to get some really good pictures of the cremation equipment and the smaller furnaces that were used for body parts that did not completely disintegrate during the first cremation process. Joe had brought a very small flashlight and would go into the rooms first, checking to make sure everything was safe and that we were not going to happen into something – or someone – dangerous. So, we made our way from room to room, shooting randomly at nothing and hoping that we did get something. We did not call out to any spirits and we did not use any electronic voice phenomenon (EVP) equipment. We only had my camera to record anything that might want to reveal itself to us. After about an hour of investigating the rundown old crematorium, we decided to head out and call it a day. As I was leaving, I stopped and shot one final shot into the darkness of the room that was right across from the furnaces. It was one picture, but out of everything I took at Eastern Cemetery that day, it is without a doubt the only one I can say came back with anything that resembled "evidence." As I sat at my computer that night going over the pictures, I was mostly disappointed that I had been unable to capture any orbs or anything. I scanned each picture, enlarging it, turning it, examining it every way I could so that I did not miss anything. That was when I looked at the last picture I took that day. As I enlarged the photo, my blood ran cold as I realized that I had captured *something* — to this day I cannot say what it is — on my camera. I enlarged the picture more and more, zooming in to make sure that what I was seeing was not a trick of the light or a figment of my over-active imagination, and,

Picture shot into completely dark room with no windows. It appears that there is a skeletal face emerging in three-dimensional form. A hand or wrist can also be detected.

Detail.

indeed it was nothing of the sort. *There was definitely something there*. Sitting at my computer, my hands began to tremble as I realized with no uncertainty that I had captured *something*. I will not speculate as to what it is that my camera caught as I shot into the darkness of Eastern Cemetery Crematorium, but what I will say is that I know what I see in the picture. You take a look and perhaps you will see the same thing I did, or, perhaps, you will come up with a better explanation than I did. I could not come up with anything reasonable to explain what I caught on my camera, but I will not rule out that this could be a ghostly entity.

The Old Pioneer Cemetery

On the night we visited Talbott Tavern and the surrounding areas, local ghost hunter Patti Starr led us to certain "hot spots" where things seemed to be most active. I had to admit I was skeptical, but willing to suspend my own disbelief for the sake of the book. It was only after returning home that I really started to get the feeling that there may just be something out there that cannot be explained. In the pictures that I took, I think what amazed me more than anything else was the way that Patti could talk to the spirits and have them do as she asked. At one point while we were out in the Pioneer Cemetery, Patti asked the spirits to appear in specific colors. At the time, that really didn't mean very much to me. It was only after I was home, looking at what I had actually captured, that my opinion really began to change.

Orbs were spotted throughout the cemetery.

Even though it's not in the best of focus due to the difficulty with lighting (and the picture is in black & white), the orbs appear in the exact colors requested, bright orange and green.

45

The lights belong to cars and a streetlight, but the large orbs are anyone's guess.

I asked my husband, Jim, "Do you remember in what colors Patti asked the spirits show themselves?"

"Yeah," he replied nonchalantly. "Bright green and bright orange."

"Look at this!" I exclaimed to him wildly. "I have them here, just like she said."

Patti told us that she asked for different colors on different occasions so that there is no mistaking what is happening, and from what I caught, I have to say that it is pretty compelling evidence.

3

The Paris Tuberculosis Hospital

C onsider for a moment that you are a child at the turn of the century and your parents have taken you to the only hospital around to be cured of consumption. You watched your brother die at home just last year. You all gathered around him in his last moments, when he was too weak to speak or to breathe. He coughed and tried to breathe, but could not catch his breath. His eyes were wide and sunken as they stared into

Looking more like an old abandoned warehouse, the Paris TB Hospital is but a shadow of its former self.

There is a filmy presence off to the left side of the old chest X-Ray machine. I cannot be certain what it is, but it did not show up on comparative photos.

the faces of those around him. Even as your parents reassure him that he will feel much better in the morning, there is the look in his eyes, the look of terror, telling you that he *knows.* He can feel death on him and you can smell it in the room. That sick smell of vomit and dried blood is one that you know oh so well. It was only after he began to cough and cough and cough that you realized that he was not going to catch his breath this time. His little body was not strong enough. This time he was going to drown to death in his own blood and all it took was looking into the ruptured blood vessels in the whites of his eyes to tell you that it was only a matter of minutes before it would all be over and the dreaded coughing would stop. Forever. At the time the sound of your mother's voice crying, "My Baby! My Baby" as she sobbed over the little five-year-old body, made your blood run cold and all you wanted to do was run away – far away – from the deathbed and the bloody bed sheets.

Comparative photo of x-ray machine.

Now, as you walk through the front doors of the looming hospital, you listen for the telltale rasp and the rattle of death. The place looks nice enough, happy enough, but you can see by the look on your mother's face that she believes she is bringing you here to die. You don't know it at the time, but in two short years, your entire family will succumb to the disease and that even in your final moments, as the doctors reassure you that you will be fine in the morning, you can feel the icy grip of terror upon you as you can't catch your breath, slowly drowning in your own blood.

The History

Doctors at the turn of the century and later knew almost immediately by listening to the complaints of the patient whether or not the patient was consumptive, a malady so named because it appeared to "consume" the person and their internal body systems, causing them to waste away. Tuberculosis (TB) was categorized into three phases, and the symptoms were very specific: weight loss, severe night sweats, rapid pulse or heart palpitations, in addition to coughing up of blood filled sputum. Emily Yoffe, in writing about Nicole Kidman's consumptive end in *Moulin Rouge,* states:

> "Although the word "tuberculosis" first appeared in 1860, it wasn't until 1882 that German physician Robert Koch identified the rod-shaped bacterium that caused the illness. While tuberculosis can affect many parts of the body, such as the bones or digestive tract, its greatest affinity is for the lungs. When actively infected people cough or sneeze, they spread droplets that can be inhaled by others. It usually takes prolonged contact to contract an infection, and even then the immune systems of healthy people can effectively contain the exposure. But in people with an active, late-stage case of TB, the lung tissue gets eaten away by rapidly expanding colonies of bacteria. Victims may experience weight loss, fever, night sweats, and coughing up of blood-filled sputum. Despite the movies, it is not a pretty way to die."[4]

The doctors knew that to die a consumptive end was to, in cases of pulmonary tuberculosis, to drown in one's own blood. One doctor wrote that:

> "The variable course of TB only served to make it more baffling and terrifying."

Physicians could not easily predict whether a consumptive patient would succumb within months, linger for years, or somehow manage to overcome the disease altogether. According to William Sweetser, a nineteenth century American physician, the first stage of consumption was marked by a dry, persistent cough, pains in the chest, and some difficulty breathing, any of which could be symptoms of less dire illnesses. The second stage brought a cough described by Dr. Sweetser as "severe, frequent, and harassing" as well as a twice-daily "hectic fever," an accelerated pulse, and a deceptively healthy ruddiness in the complexion.

In the final, fatal stage, wrote the doctor, "the emaciation is frightful and the most mournful change is witnessed...the cheeks are hollow...rendering the expression harsh and painful. The eyes are commonly sunken in their sockets...and often look morbidly bright and staring." At this point, throat ulcers made eating difficult and speech was limited to a hoarse whisper. Once the distinctive "graveyard cough" began, diagnosis was certain and death inevitable. Rarely, wrote Dr. Sweetser, "life, wasted to the most feeble spark, goes out almost insensibly." More typically, severe stomach cramps, excessive sweating, a choking sensation, and vomiting of blood preceded the victim's demise."[5]

People mistakenly believe that Tuberculosis is a modern affliction, the fodder upon which the romance writers built much of their plot lines. It is the pathetic end to *Camille*, by Alexander Dumas (pere). It's the death of the little girl who curls up next to Jane in the book *Jane Eyre.* It's Nicole Kidman coughing up blood at the end of *Moulin Rouge.* It's the final, heart-wrenching scene of the opera "La Boheme." There is no end to the stories that incorporate the long, drawn out dying process of their main character by afflicting him, but usually her, with consumption — more commonly known as TB. It must be observed, however, that there are reasons for this. The art of a society or culture will reflect its values, morals, beliefs, and, more often than not, its social afflictions. It is small wonder that so many novels, operas, or any form of visual and representative arts focus on the death sentence of TB. However, the misconception is that TB was a new disease. There is actual evidence now that the earliest human, also known as *homo erectus*, who was found outside of Turkey, was plagued with and likely died from a form of TB that infected the meninges in the brain, Leptominingitis tuberculosa. This form of TB was not as common as the kind that affected the lungs, but still as fatal. This was found in a human specimen that was over 500,000 years old! Tuberculosis was present as far back as Rome, the Vikings, and ran rampantly into the twentieth century. It was for this reason that facilities such as Waverly Hills were constructed.

Tuberculosis has been called the "White Death" from the massive numbers who died of the disease through the years, pitting it against the "Black Death" or Bubonic Plague that ravaged Europe in the 1300s. At the turn of the century it was responsible for one out of every five deaths. TB is a wasting disease, an insidious monster that struck with impartiality. Old and young, rich and poor—all who contracted consumption had chances for recovery that were small at best. Tuberculosis is a highly contagious disease that is spread primarily through coughing and sneezing. The disease is present in tiny sputum particles and not everyone who is exposed to the disease actually contracts it. The strength of a person's immune system is mostly responsible for whether or not the disease becomes active. This could explain why doctors and nurses were able to work with patients day after day and not always contract the disease. One hypothesis is that by working with the disease day after day, their immune systems were strengthened and they avoided becoming infected with an active form of TB.

The Hospital Building Today

Looming like an immense brick reminder of the pain and suffering that comes with disease, the former Tuberculosis hospital in Paris, Kentucky is an overlooked and forgotten memory of the past. As I drove to meet Dave and Tommy Jones of the Kentucky Area Paranormal Society (KAPS), I was a little nervous about rummaging through a place that was completely deserted and very dangerous due to the severe disrepair of the building. Dave had prepped me on some of the history of the building. A former local law enforcement officer, Dave now spends his time investigating the paranormal and locations that are supposedly haunted. Extremely attentive to detail and dedicated to debunking "fake" locations, sightings, and experiences, when Dave told me that he was certain the old hospital was haunted, I believed him. Ethical to the highest degree, Dave and his group accepts no money from outside sources that they help. KAPS offers a service to those in need, those who are bothered by *otherworldly* happenings. Dave and his group adhere to a strict code of conduct lest their impeccable reputation be marred by any negativity. In short, I respected Dave and his group from the beginning and if they said the hospital was haunted, that was good enough for me.

The TB hospital in Paris does not enjoy nearly as much notoriety as Waverly Hills in Louisville. Like a quiet little sister living in the shadow of the family beauty queen, the hospital in Paris stands today lonely, deserted, with broken windows, and asbestos insulation falling all around the interior. Driving up the long road to get to the top of the hill where the hospital was located, I could almost imagine being a child, seeing this for the first time. Did they know that they were coming there to do one of two things, die or get better? I wondered how the parents felt when they had to leave their little ones behind, not knowing what was going to happen to them or if they themselves would be the next patients. The sadness was immense and I could feel it all over that building, not because I am overly sentient or prone to feelings of ESP, but because I am a mother and I can only imagine the horror and the real life suffering of the people who visited their children here regularly, many for the last time.

When I first entered the building, temperatures were below zero, so finding a "cold spot" was extremely difficult. What amazed me from the outset was that the very first room I encountered was the morgue. When I stepped into the room, my camera, fully charged, refused to work at all. I checked and double-checked, frustrated that perhaps my camera was faulty. Dave just laughed and said that this was very normal. Energy drains are common in places of extreme paranormal activity, very likely because the spirits themselves are energy and will drain it from anyplace they can. The table on which the bodies were laid was pulled out and I was able to take some really good pictures of the room itself. From the moment we walked in, doors began to slam. While Dave and Tommy were setting up their workstation in what was formerly a nurses' greeting area, I took pictures. Freezing and already beginning to feel the numbness creep into my hands, I looked around. Due to exposed wires and elevators that were now just empty shafts, I soon decided to leave the tour to the experts who were familiar with the building.

The event that had prompted me to visit the hospital was an incident that KAPS had caught on tape on their last visit to the hospital. Their voice recorder had captured the voice of a man who said his name was "Ian." When they stopped in front of a huge, heavy wooden door, the door swung open on its own. When they shut it and asked for it to be opened again, Ian complied. This video may still be seen on their website www.kapsonline.com. It is well worth a look or two. We made our way to that particular door and nothing happened that day. Doors all around us were slamming shut and we could hear them resonating throughout the abandoned hospital, but I could not rule out that this was just the wind sweeping through the halls. It was, however, unnerving. It was not until I was in a room by myself that I actually saw something. I was taking pictures when something moved past me and down the hall. I was about five feet away, but I called out to Jim, thinking that he had come looking for me. When I got no reply at all, I panicked, because there was most certainly someone there. I

Ian's door.

This was the last shot of the day. Is there a man staring out of the top window down at us? Perhaps this is a doctor, because he appears to have a clipboard in his hand or his arm is resting on a window ledge.

Detail of Top Window.

sprinted from the room, calling up and down the hall for Dave, Tommy, or Jim. No one answered. It was not until I made my way out of the deserted wing that I realized that everyone was either on another floor or way down at the other end of the hospital ward. By that time, I was shaking — and not from the cold. I caught up with the boys and stayed with them pretty closely for the rest of the investigation. That day was pretty quiet and I had to admit that other than the slamming doors and the person who passed me in the deserted hall, I had not seen much else. That does not mean that it's not haunted. There is way too much evidence gathered by the guys from KAPS to think that it's not. However, what I did experience that day was good enough for me. Even though the only picture I was able to take that had something "anomalous" in it was the last picture I took, I agree with Dave and Tommy about the activity in the building and look forward to going there again...when the weather is warmer!

The Morgue. This was the last stop for many people who stayed here. I couldn't help but be sadden by the thought of the little children who laid here.

4

Joe's Older Than Dirt Cafe

Tragedy seems to be the common denominator among many of the haunted locations I have visited. Stories of those who loved, died, or were tragically taken before they felt their time had come are the fodder upon which many investigators and thrill seekers surfeit themselves, never quite getting their fill. It came as a pleasant surprise for me then to happen upon this quaint little restaurant on New LaGrange Road in Louisville. From the exterior decorations of life-size moose and swine (artificial of course), to the myriad taxidermied-animals dressed in party hats and cummerbunds (real, of course) on the interior, Joe's is obviously a place for those who are in the mood for a good meal or who just want to thumb their nose at the PETA people. Lively and fun, even in the early afternoon hours, Joe's is an interesting mix of old and new. From the old tree that grows straight through the restaurant's floor and reaches the ceiling, to the lodge-like atmosphere of the sitting area, Joe's — and the Gishes — welcome the community with great food and décor that one could look at for hours and still never be satisfied. When I interviewed Janet, she was more than willing to share some of her own prior experiences, as well as what she knows and has personally witnessed at the restaurant. While the restaurant itself may not be steeped in personal tragedy, Janet and Gary certainly have seen their share of it.

One of nine children, Janet comes from a very close family. Their father owned and operated the J. T. Nelson Company, a manufacturing

The original Joe.

business that made doors for railcars, and Gary and Janet were the prior owners of "Tootsies," a shoe store that they gave up for the Café they currently own. Their extensive knowledge of business and love of family shows throughout the café, mostly in the form of old pictures of family members that are strategically placed throughout. However, no family is without its share of horror stories or tragic events. When I asked Janet if she had been "sensitive" to paranormal happenings early on in life, she smiled sadly and I knew that I already had my answer. As it had been explained to me, people who often see or encounter paranormal activity have done so for a long time.

We sat and Janet told me the story of her own brush with the spirit world. The family had planned a vacation to New Orleans one year. The rest of the family members were packed and ready to go, but Janet was very reluctant to get everything ready to head out. Something inside her, she explained, told her that there would be no vacation this year. Up to the day they were supposed to leave, Janet had not packed her bags. All that day she knew she was supposed to get ready and have everything packed, but there was a nagging *knowledge* deep within that told her something was not right. As she explained it, she knew her younger brother, Mark, had been murdered. She said, "The knowledge was 'I am dead.'" All through the evening this voice inside her warned her that Mark was not with them anymore, so it did not come as any surprise when her niece called Gary, her husband, and told them that they had to go home immediately.

> "Mark's been shot and killed."
> To which Janet replied, "I know."
> "Who told you?"
> "Mark did."

Mark was only twenty years old and this could have been his last contact with the family he loved so dearly. Not long after that incident, Janet's sister Donna was in the family kitchen with her boyfriend, Andy. As clearly as could be heard, a voice called out "Donny!"— which was Mark's own private pet name for his sister. While death and tragedy bring about strange actions and reactions in the lives of those who are left behind, it cannot be denied that incidents such as these are more than mere coincidence or the products of overactive imaginations. Surely, beyond the limits of this finite world, Mark was trying to reach out to his family one last time.

After listening to Janet recount numerous stories about her family and her own experiences within the restaurant, I was anxious to start poking around myself. I looked around and shot pictures to my heart's content — that is until my camera decided that there were certain areas where it simply would not work. I have to say that my battery was full and that I had to keep recharging it several times in order to finish the interview and the photo shoot. I noted in my journal that there were four spots where my camera refused to work: the bar area, liquor room, bathroom, and the old bar area. I had to go back, charge my camera, and try to finish shooting, only to give up when I realized that this phenomenon was what several people had warned me about. They said not to be surprised if my camera or any other battery operated equipment failed at times. Energy can be drained quite easily and often one finds that a camera that is fully charged and in good working order one minute, will be unable to function the next. I finally gave up on those areas later that afternoon.

Without a doubt, the most famous paranormal patron of Joe's is the entity Janet refers to as the "Man in the Red Plaid Shirt." While sounding like the title of a b-rated Steve Martin movie, this man is a real presence in the establishment, and it is believed that he might even be the original "Joe." One day when Janet was opening up the restaurant, she came around a corner and was stunned to see an older man standing behind the bar. He had great detail about him and was dressed as someone might have been in the 1940s or 50s. He was a tall man, tall enough that you could see him from the waist up. But, the most striking thing about him was his red plaid shirt. Sightings of "Joe" are not unusual and are, in fact, common. He has been seen behind the bar numerous times, as

The favorite spot for the Man in the Red Plaid Shirt.

A partial shot of the old bar area.

well as in the kitchen area, the service alley, and the "old bar." The sightings in the "old bar" area would not be unusual since before the establishment became what it is today, it once functioned as the original home of Joe and his family. Where the old bar stands today was once Joe's bedroom. It has been speculated that spirits cannot understand when renovations are done and continually trace the path or go to the places that existed, as they knew them in life. A wall could stand where a door once was. The spirit will not see the wall, but pass through it as if the door still existed as it did when he or she used to walk through it. Perhaps, the Man in the Red Plaid Shirt is continuing to re-trace the steps he knew so well in life and the bar is simply where his living quarters once were. In any case, there have been so many sightings of him that it cannot be dismissed very easily.

Janet took me to the room where the liquor is stored and told me a story before she opened the door. She was standing then, just as we were now, in front of a large, wooden door that must be accessed by a key. She put the key in the lock and turned it, not expecting to find any resistance. However, when she attempted to

There have been many complaints about noises and activity in the ladies restroom. This could be a reflection, but I don't have to try very hard to see a face in that mirror.

push the door open, it abruptly pushed back, shutting on her from the inside. Thinking that someone was playing a joke, she opened it again and turned on the light, only to find that it was dark and there was no one there. It is not a heavy door, I found, as I pushed it open myself. There were no windows or doors that could have caused a draft or a sudden surge of resistance. So what was pushing back at her, teasing her in its own way? No one can be certain, but she feels that whatever it was, it was not meant to hurt or frighten her. It may have just wanted a little attention.

Whether the presence inside Joe's Older than Dirt Café is the presence of Joe or some of his former patrons, one thing can be said. In addition to being a wonderful a place to come for lunch or dinner, the restaurant holds a great amount of history for those who love the area. And, it would appear, that sometimes it is very difficult to leave that which we love and are familiar with. Outside of having difficulty with my camera, I did not catch very much that morning, but the photos that did show up with a few strange things are worth taking a second or third glance.

5

Phoenix Hill Tavern

The Roof Garden decorated for Mardi Gras.

Date: January 26, 2008, 7:00 p.m.

At this very moment I am breathless and sitting at the bar in the area known as the "Tap Room." I have just encountered several things that I, skeptic that I am, cannot explain for the life of me. I usually start out my chapters with the history, but I had to capture this moment and the rush I feel in it. I am not sure of the history of Phoenix Hill Tavern at the very moment I am writing this introduction, *but what I do know is this—for a person who does not believe in ghosts at this very moment I **AM** pretty darn convinced. When I began this project, I could not honestly say for sure that there was anything left of a person after this life. Perhaps, like a memory, we exist for awhile, living and loving those people whom we cannot bear to let go. I thought perhaps that we might hover in the grey realms, like a lucid dream that gives us the ability to fly for a moment and then we wake in a place filled with the beliefs of the Judeo-Christian world. However, I must admit that up to this very moment I have never come face-to-face with anything remotely "supernatural." But, I cannot deny what I saw with my own eyes and captured with my own camera.* (Note from personal journal written after the encounter in the second floor ladies bathroom)

The History

O riginally known as "Preston's Enlargement," the area where Phoenix Hill is located is right across from another entry in this book, Eastern Cemetery. Known for its showcasing of local talent and the gorgeous roof garden, which puts one in mind of the Hanging Gardens of Babylon, Phoenix Hill is nestled in an eclectic district of Louisville that was once owned by local gentry and plantation owner, William Preston. Annexed by the city of Louisville in 1827, Phoenix Hill was a booming district inhabited by many German immigrants who came in and settled in the shotgun style homes that line the streets. The Tavern itself dates back to the pre-prohibition era and has always functioned as a place to buy spirits of the more potable persuasion. Hovering over its illustrious history as a building that is inseparable from our city as a landmark is its reputation as a haunted local haunt. People who visit are surprised to find themselves face to face with the "Lady on the Stairs" or in the middle of a cold spot on a hot summer day.

Recently remodeled to accommodate the new smoking ban in Louisville, the one major area of the bar now sports an "open roof" where everyone can have a drink – or a smoke – under the stars. It appears, however, that not everyone is happy about the recent renovations and the activity inside Phoenix Hill Tavern would attest to that fact.

Early in the evening of January 26, 2008, I took a chance and decided to just show up at Phoenix Hill and kindly ask the management to just let me have a look around, take a few pictures, and maybe talk to some people who work there. Most people, when they hear that you would like to talk to them about being in a book, are pretty great about giving interviews. The great folks at Phoenix Hill went above and beyond anything I had anticipated. Even though I have lived in Louisville all my life, I had never experienced Phoenix Hill Tavern and the great ambience for which it is famous. As I walked in, the exposed brick reminded me of the interior of a prohibition-era speakeasy and the warm smell of baking appetizers made my stomach growl. I wondered if I could just sit around and munch, but knowing that I was in possibly one of the oldest and most haunted places around made me hungrier to start talking to the people and taking pictures.

Jeanette Gray and Frankie Rogers, a beautiful mother/daughter management team, displayed graciousness and hospitality, pretty much letting me have the run of the place before the bands began that evening. No strangers to local ghost hunters, Frankie and Jeanette were used to people coming in with meters and gizmos that cost more than my first car. I explained that I was not a "ghost hunter" and I was not coming to track anything down or stir anything up. As a writer, I try my best to tell good stories and I was anxious to hear about the goings-on in the Tavern. If I captured anything on my camera, so much the better, but I came into the evening expecting to find diddlysquat and hopefully, I elaborated further, would be sorely disappointed in that area. As it turned out, Phoenix Hill has, up to this point, given me some of the best pictures of anomalies that I have ever taken.

Employees are usually the ones who see the strange happenings behind the scenes, hearing the music or the voices that linger long after the customers are gone and the bar is shut down for the night. Nick Ford, one of the security guards at the Tavern, can attest to the fact that even before I visited that evening, strange things do happen — often. Standing a good six feet tall or more, Nick is not a man that anyone, living or otherwise, would take lightly. His stature makes him a real force to be reckoned with and he was not shy about telling me that one of the eeriest places in the entire bar is the roof garden.

"You can come in and be by yourself," he explained "and know that you are not alone up here. You can see people moving in the darkness, even when you know there isn't anyone there."

As I walked around the open area, I noticed the plants and trees that seem to grow out of the very brick itself. Beautiful and yet deceptively quiet, I shot many pictures around the roof garden and didn't really see anything on them that would make me stop and take a second look. However, my feeling of unease in the mostly deserted area grew with every corner I took and I sheepishly asked Nick if he would follow me around, as I am somewhat of a chicken when it comes to going into strange places alone. We made our way around the roof garden and stopped in an area that was partitioned off by a heavy canvas curtain. I asked to shoot some pictures behind the canvas and Nick explained that it was just an area where the bands kept their equipment before a show. I decided to take a position where I would be in the shadow so that I would not compromise the pictures I was taking. The very first picture I shot simply took my breath away. On my camera it would appear that an entity, often known as a "shadow person," was directly in front of me. I shot a few other pictures from the same position so that I would know that it was not a trick of the light or something I had done, and truly, what showed up on the first picture was not seen on any of the others. When I looked

In this picture, I was not backlit nor was I standing anywhere that would cast a shadow. From what I have been told, it appears that this could be a "shadow person." It appears as if that whatever...it's holding out a tray. In comparative shots, this figure never emerged again.

at the digital image, I yelped a bit, more out of excitement than fear, which brought Nick over immediately.

"Look! Look! Is this what I think it is?" I amateurishly screeched as Nick got really excited and joined in my enthusiasm.

"It looks like a shadow person to me!" he exclaimed, as we reveled in the fact that I had caught at least one good picture on this expedition.

"Let's go take some more!"

Elated and invigorated by my "find" I followed Nick back through the roof garden and into the taproom. We mounted the stairs that the "Lady" was known to have traveled and then we abruptly stopped in front of the second floor ladies bathroom. The wonderful thing about digital photography, I personally think, is the immediacy in which you can see what you have just shot. I was still flying high having captured my first shadow person, which would have made the entire evening worthwhile if I had shot nothing else. What lay in store for me in that bathroom, however, was one of the most incredible things I have ever witnessed. Nick explained, as he opened the door to the Victorian decorated ladies room, that many strange things had been seen and heard in the bathroom. I went in and had a look around. A good piece of advice that Patti Starr, a ghost hunter from Bardstown, Kentucky, gave me was that televisions and mirrors were great objects to shoot. She said that it is easy to catch faces in reflective surfaces, so I took her at her word and began to shoot at the television. As I stepped closer to the back of the ladies room, I heard a sound. It was as if someone had thumped the metal garbage can under the paper towel dispenser.

"Nick?" No answer. "Nick?"

I started to get a little unnerved and made my way back toward the door, which I noticed he was still holding open.

"Did you do that?"

"Do what?"

"Didn't you hear that sound? I thought you were throwing something away."

"Nope. Not me."

At that point, he stepped inside the ladies room and let the door close. At that moment, a door to the first stall, which was no more than three feet from either of us, slammed shut. Jumping out of our skins, he raced for the door and so did I.

"What the hell?!" he said.

"Did you see what I saw?"

"See it? I felt it. Something pulled my hair."

"Ok. I'm going back in."

Breathless and on an endorphin induced high, I promptly went back in and Nick stayed, holding the door. I told him I was going to shoot some pictures into the mirror and see if anything turned up. The very first picture yielded a nice orb to the left of me — right in front of the first stall. Fortunately, I have a rapid shoot mechanism on my camera, and I was able to take multiple shots, quickly.

"Nick. Look at this."

"What is IT?"

"I don't know…but IT'S moving."

I watched the screen of my camera as picture after picture showed the orb in motion. Patti had also told me that you have to be careful when shooting orbs because many are just dust or water particles that people want to believe are orbs. I remembered her advice when she said, "Ask the orb to appear in a color or to do something like come sit in your hand. If it will obey a request, you know that it is not just dust."

After ten or twenty pictures and some very easy speaking to this thing, I held out my hand like she had shown me. I kindly requested that the orb come sit in my hand and I shot frame after frame, watching this thing come closer and closer until it did exactly that. What I did not expect, however, was what came next. As I shot the pictures and the orb hovered in my hand, I looked at my screen and could not believe what I saw. The orb had *MANIFESTED* itself into a partial apparition that appeared to be looking over my shoulder at my

There is a definite white, filmy orb to the left, hanging above the plants.

camera screen. Folks, I can tell you in all honesty that this skeptical gal just about jumped out of her skin when she saw that. Nick and I took the camera, hooting with glee and went to show Jeanette and Frankie what just happened. By this time, the whole place was abuzz with employee activity and everyone was excited to see something that they *knew* was there, captured for everyone to see.

I went to several other places, but there was no place that was as active as that bathroom. Later that evening, I wondered to myself if it was active because there was the male presence in there or if it is always there and just wanted to take the opportunity to present itself. In either case, those who might have been skeptics before, this old girl included, were made believers.

So who are these people who continue to hang around Phoenix Hill Tavern, even after they have passed? Some people think that it might be the original owners, coming in just as they did in life. Perhaps, like the Lady on the Stairs, this was a place of familiarity and comfort. Even in life we tend to want to be in places where life is being lived to the fullest and where people are enjoying themselves. If we didn't, the state fairs would be empty and no one would ever come back to the places where "everybody knows your name" — to coin a famous phrase. Are these entities patrons who just can't let go of their favorite hangout? It's anyone's guess. I suppose I could bring in monitors to capture voices or gauge temperature changes in the room, but in the end, it all ends the same. We suspend our own disbelief in such matters, clinging to the evidence that provides us with proof that there is something more that exists after this life ends. Those who refuse to believe that will always believe that, no matter how much evidence exists or how many orbs or voices are caught on tape. Like religion, believing is a choice and those who choose *not* to believe, would never be convinced anyway. But for Nick, myself, and the dozens of other employees who saw what we saw that night, disbelief gets harder and harder to hold onto.

EDITOR'S NOTE:

Pictures of the traveling orb begin on the next page.

"I shot into a mirror and the orb thing showed up. I took a series of pictures where the thing moved and actually responded to me asking it to come sit in my hand. In one picture, it appears behind me and the head and shoulders can be seen. It actually follows the two men out of the bathroom and then appears as a more transparent orb in the hallway.

If you watch them in sequence, you will see the Bouncer looking over my shoulder because he can't believe what he's seeing. I'm giving you, the readers, carte blanche to these photos and share with me what you think it is.

In images 10 through 13, I ask it to sit in my hand and it comes pretty close.

Image 14 is where you can see a figure behind me.

Images 15, 16, and 17 are comparative shots. I left the bathroom and came back to try to recreate what had happened. Nothing showed up in these shots.

In image 18, the orb is following the men out into the hall.

In image 19, I'M following the orb out into the hall.

Image 20 is the same hall one second later. Comparative photo.

1

2

3

4

5

6

7

8

9

10

11

12

13

14

15

16

17

18

19

20

Bobby Mackey's Music World

*D*uring the course of writing this book I have discovered many things about man's inhumanity to man. Horrific as it may be, the stories of untimely deaths that leave disembodied spirits lingering in the realm of the living are as common as the places they continue to haunt. I can honestly say, however, that the stories that accompany the tales of the haunting of Bobby Mackey's Music World in Wilder, Kentucky, are some of the most disturbing tales I have ever heard. To understand why it is that this place continues to turn up on the Who's Who of Haunted Locations, the story of Pearl Bryan, Alonzo Walling, and Scott Jackson must be told. After hours of research and hundreds of pages of first hand accounts, I finally believe I have enough information to do this story more justice than those stories that would gloss over the gory details and leave the truth as buried and forgotten as Pearl's headless body.

Murder, Gangsters, Suicide, and Devil Worship

The Ballad of Pearl Bryan

Young girls, if you'll listen, a story I'll relate
That happened near Fort Thomas in the old Kentucky State
On January the thirty-first the dreadful deed was done
By Jackson and by Walling; how cold Pearl's blood did run!

But little did her parents think when she left her happy home,
Their darling girl just in her youth would never more return.
How sad it would have been to them to have heard Pearl's lonely voice
At midnight in that lonely spot where those two boys rejoiced!

And little did Pearl Bryan think when she left her home
The grip she carried in her hand would hide her head away
She thought it was her lover's hand she could trust both night and day
Although it was her lover's hand that took her life away

The driver in the seat is all who tells of Pearl's sad fate
Of poor Pearl Bryan away from home in the old Kentucky state
Of her aged parents we all know well what a fortune they would give
If Pearl could but to them return her natural life to live

In came Pearl Bryan's sister and falling to her knees
Begging to Scott Jackson, "My sister's head, O please!"
Scott Jackson he set stubborn not a word would he proclaim
"I'll meet my sister in heaven, where I'll find her missing head."

In came Walling's mother, Pleading for her son
"Don't take my son, my only son; from him I cannot part
O please don't take him to prison; it would break my poor old heart!"

The jury gave a verdict, and to their feet they sprung:
"For the crime these boys committed they surely must be hung."

(Author's note: This old ballad was found at Mudcat.org, which states the song is from a book of traditional folk ballads compiled by A. Friedman and published by Penguin Books. The web site is http://supersearch. mudcat.org/@displaysong.cfm?SongID=4632)

The Tangled Web of Pearl, Scott, and Alonzo

Pearl Bryan was a lovely young woman from Greencastle, Indiana, who trusted, as many people do, someone who would disappoint and betray her. The daughter of a prominent farmer, Pearl was blessed with grace, beauty, and the oddly identifiable feature of having webbed toes. The Bryans were an old family who had been in the area for generations and boasted an excellent standing in the Greencastle community in 1896. Pearl was the youngest of seven children and the favorite of her parents. Graduating from high school with honors, the parents had high hopes of their daughter making a good match, socially and economically. She was the belle of the county and the object of affection for all the local young men, including her second cousin, William (Billy) Wood. The two had become very close, as the families only lived a short distance from each other, and rumors had run amok about an illicit relationship between the two, but that was dispelled during the course of the trial, in which William became a prime suspect. She was quite accomplished and had no lack of suitors for her affections, yet she had the innocence that goes with the typical image of the midwestern farmer's daughter. William was often seen in her company and the two enjoyed an intimate friendship in place of the romantic relationship that he might have desired; yet it would be revealed over the course of time and during the trial that the most dangerous acquaintance he would ever make would eventually lead to Pearl's death.

William Wood lived very near to the home of a family by the name of Jackson. Mrs. Jackson was a decent lady who had a son near to the age of William and who had gone out from Greencastle to study at the school of dentistry at DePauw. The two young men struck up a friendship and over the course of time, William introduced Scott Jackson to his lovely cousin, Pearl. Pearl was immediately thunderstruck by the handsome young Jackson and not knowing anything about his past, the two began to "keep company." However, had she known at the time that Jackson was a petty criminal who had already been indicted for embezzling $32,00 from his former employer, she might have thought twice about entertaining thoughts of a future with him. Scott Jackson, whose family originally hailed from New Jersey, and a fellow employee, had embezzled the money from the railroad company they worked for and were only discovered when they began making huge bets at the local racetrack — and winning. When investigated, Scott Jackson turned state's evidence against his associate and was promptly released. His partner in crime, however, went to prison to serve out his sentence.

Scott Jackson and his mother then moved to Greencastle, Indiana, where they started over with no talk of his former crime hanging over his head. This would prove to be a damning piece of evidence when it came to the murder trial, as it was theorized that Scott was again attempting to commit the crime and then pin the guilt on someone else. Sociopathic behavior appeared to surface quite early in his life, and Scott would exhibit this throughout the course of events over the next year. Yet, no one in the sleepy little town of Greencastle saw anything except what Scott Jackson wanted them to see, which was that he was a fine, upstanding young man who would make a fine dentist one day. Any girl in the county would be lucky to have him as her suitor, yet he set his sights on Pearl Bryan.

Pearl and Scott's relationship soon blossomed from friendship to intimacy. As young men often do, one can imagine the things he promised her and the dreams that they shared about the future. One piece of evidence cannot be denied, however, and that was that in 1886, Pearl found out that she was pregnant by Jackson. In that day and age, the blot on the Bryan family would have been disgraceful and Pearl was frightened, to be sure. By the time the decision was made that Pearl would have to do something, she was already four or five months pregnant, according to the postmortem examination. She realized that something must be done, and that Jackson was completely uninterested in proposing matrimony. She was just another girl in a string of many and Jackson's only thought was how to rid himself of the problem of Pearl Bryan. Panicked, Pearl confided in her friend and cousin, William Wood. After speaking to Jackson and to Pearl, it was decided that Pearl should come to Cincinnati, Ohio, to have an abortion, which was supposed to be performed by either Jackson or his new roommate, Alonzo Walling. She had been told that an old lady who was quite skilled in these matters would be performing the procedure, so there was very little for her to fear. She did not know at the time that everything she had been told to this point had been a lie. Jackson had no intention of helping her out of the precarious situation she was in anymore than he did of marrying the unfortunate young girl. According to the records I found, she did not have any hope that he would marry her, nor did she attempt to trap him into matrimony. This would appear to be the case of misplaced loyalty, yet there is no indication that she expected anything from him other than help out of trouble.

The Murder

Knowing that the time was coming fast when she would no longer be able to hide her pregnancy, Pearl agreed to meet Scott Jackson in Cincinnati. She told her family that she was going to visit some friends in Indianapolis and set off by herself. We will never know if Pearl was frightened to travel alone or if she was reluctant about the impending surgery. We will never know if she was secretly hoping Jackson would change his mind or if hers was just set to do the deed she felt she must do. What we do know is that Pearl arrived in

Cincinnati on Tuesday, January 28, 1896, by train. We know that she carried a medium sized alligator skin valise (suitcase) with her and that she was taken to a local hotel called the Indiana House. Jackson had, according to Walling, asked him to help a girl he knew out of "trouble." Walling agreed to help. At the local saloon, the Wallinghouse, Jackson had asked a few of his buddies from medical school about different poisons and which would kill the quickest. It was never his intention to help Pearl have an abortion. From the testimonies of others during the trial, he had always intended to kill her and hide the body. One of his original plans was to kill her in the room where she was staying and just leave the body. However, his next plan, according to testimony by Walling, was to kill her somewhere else, dismember her, and drop the pieces of the body in various "vaults" around town. For reasons unknown, this did not happen. Instead, it appears that the crime happened thus, according to the 1898 account in the Kentucky Virtual Library:

> Jackson administered four grains of cocaine mixed with sixteen drops of water. This was supposed to paralyze Pearl's vocal chords so she could not cry or call for help. The two men then hired a "hack" or cab, to take them out to a remote location. The cab driver left the scene, leaving the two men behind. Once alone, Jackson and Walling took Pearl to the farm of a man named James Locke, who lived in the Kentucky town of Fort Thomas. It had not started to rain at that time, but would later on in the evening, washing away evidence. Pearl was taken out of the cab. There are speculations that she was dead at the time or died on the trip out. However, according to a post-mortem exam record, her hands show defensive wounds, where she had tried to fight off her killer(s). So, it's fairly certain that while drugged, Pearl was most definitely alive when she made her way along the grassy banks, likely following Walling and Jackson. There were footprints in the mud that showed she walked next to the men before the struggle

ensued. At some point, Jackson turned on Pearl, ripping parts of her dress off, tearing away even the corset she was wearing. Upon finding the body, the general consensus was that she had been raped first, because of the tearing of the clothes and the fact that her dress was pulled up around her waist. However, the autopsy gave no indication of that. It likely was disarrayed during the struggle for her life. In her drugged state, she was no match for her attacker. He cut her across the throat in one clean slice, causing exsanguination. As she lay there, bleeding to death, the killer, while she was still alive, severed her head from her body at the fifth cervical vertebrae. From the way the blood pooled, it was determined that she was still alive when this happened. Jackson then took her head and put it in the suitcase she had with her, the alligator bag. Leaving the scene of the crime, the men went back into town and disposed of certain pieces of evidence, such as a bloody jacket belonging to Jackson, and pieces of clothing that Pearl had brought with her.

✝✝✝✝✝✝✝✝✝✝✝✝✝✝✝✝✝✝✝✝✝

After the body was discovered early in the morning of February 1, 1896, the authorities had a very difficult time identifying it, since there were few missing persons in the area and Pearl was from out of town. Her parents had not reported her missing, since they still believed she was visiting friends in Indianapolis. People filed in from all over trying to identify the body. Curiosity seekers and those who wanted to catch a glimpse of the macabre scene would make up stories about having missing relatives in order to glimpse the headless corpse of Pearl Bryan. None panned out as true. At the post mortem, it was discovered that the body was indeed pregnant, about four or five months along. The baby was removed and sent to the local apothecary, where it was placed in a jar of alcohol, along with her stomach, so that tests could be run to see if there were any poisons or drugs therein. The local authorities followed up all leads that could identify the body they had in their morgue, but no one knew who the girl was — just as Jackson and Walling had hoped it would be. However, the wheels of justice grind slowly, but they certainly grind. The headless corpse had a pair of shoes that were stamped with Greencastle, Indiana, and a serial number. It did not take long for the authorities to track down the shop where they had been sold and with the exact measurements of the shoe, to whom they had been sold. Once it had been determined who was the likely match to the body, they visited the home of the family, where articles of clothing were positively identified as those belonging to Pearl Bryan. Her dress had been made for a sister who had died and then made over again for Pearl. The glove was a match. However, it was the positive identification of the specific deformity of her feet that gave the family closure as to what happened to Pearl. It was only a matter of time until her death was traced back to her relationship to Scott Jackson. While he attempted to pin the death on Walling, just as he had pinned the theft so many years earlier on his accomplice, it was without a doubt Scott Jackson who master-minded the plot. While Walling may have not actively participated in the actual murder, he was aware of what happened and most definitely there on the night she died.

The Head

While all this makes for a really interesting read, two questions remain. What happened to Pearl's head and how does this relate to Bobby Mackey's Music World?

The story must unfold in its entirety to understand the first question. After Jackson and Walling left Pearl's body, they took the head back with them to Wallinghouse Saloon and left the suitcase in the care of the owner of the saloon. The next day when they went to pick it up, they disposed

The well room where Pearl's head was very likely thrown. You can still see where the floor boards have been torn away and the well exposed.

of the head. The suitcase, still on exhibit in the Campbell County Courthouse today, still has blood inside it, just as it did when authorities confiscated it in 1896. According to testimony, Walling said Jackson probably buried the head or threw it into the Ohio River. Jackson never gave any indication that this was true or false, but legend has it that they took the head across the river to the sight of an old, abandoned slaughterhouse and threw the head down an old well. Since everyone far and wide across the county looked for the head, this would make sense. The bloody clothes that were worn by Walling and Jackson were recovered from the sewers, as were Pearl's. The suitcase that held her head was recovered and used as evidence. However, the head was the one thing that remained missing and still holds the greatest mystery. Even as Walling and Jackson were facing death on the morning of their executions, neither would disclose the location of Pearl's head. Walling was all but promised a reprieve if he would only tell the family where to find it, and still he refused or either

The actual well as it looks today. Even filled in and covered over, you get a very eerie feeling standing next to it because you know what lies at the bottom.

had no clue where Jackson had really put it. They went to the scaffold, both proclaiming their innocence and neither willing to disclose that final piece of information. They received the dubious honor of being the last two men hanged in Campbell County, both protesting that the other did it. When the trap door sprung, it took both men about ten minutes to die, as their necks were not mercifully broken in the drop. Pearl's family tried to go on with their lives and forget the tragedy, as did the small town of Fort Thomas.

Even after the trial and the hangings were over, people looked far and wide for Pearl's head, although the police had real suspicions that Walling and Jackson had thrown it down into an old abandoned well on the sight where a slaughterhouse used to be. I am not sure why the well wasn't torn apart looking for the girl's head. Today, such a clue would not be ignored. We must remember that nineteenth century forensics were not what we have today and the police may not have wanted nor been able to accomplish such a feat with the resources they had at that time. What became the driving force behind their frenzy was positively identifying the body and then bringing the killers to justice. That must be done in order to provide the community and the family with a sense of closure to the entire ordeal. In the end, Pearl's body was taken back to Greencastle County where her body lies in Forest Hill Cemetery to this day. She was twenty-two years old. According to tradition, if you visit the grave of Pearl Bryan, you must leave a new Lincoln head penny on her grave so that she will not be without one on Judgment Day.

Through the years new structures were built where the slaughterhouse once stood and the well was forgotten. No excavations were done there, likely due to the fact that many were ready to forget the horrible murder and all that went with it. On that location a casino was later built. It was called the "Latin Quarter" and would later turn into a Country Western bar called Bobby Mackey's Music World. However, the story does not end there. It only takes more deadly twists and turns.

The Primrose Club and the story of Johanna

Land does not lay fallow for very long along a river because of the promise of river traffic and trade. Economic developments usually prosper and for this reason the piece of land where the slaughterhouse once stood was purchased and a casino/bingo parlor was built. Named the "Latin Quarter," only the legend of Pearl's head remained as time marched on and the community of Wilder, Kentucky – the supposed sight where Pearl's head remained, lost at the bottom of a well – was happy to forget about the tragedy that Fort Thomas thought would haunt it forever. Money must be made and at the turn of the century in pre-prohibition era Kentucky, the river would prove to be a prime location for a casino and later for organized crime. Unfortunately, the only surviving evidence of the gaming and bingo days are the old bingo boards, papers, and files that litter the basement of Bobby Mackey's Music World. Still left pretty much intact and untouched, they give evidence of the activities that went on there, but do not add to the stories of the haunting. There is one piece of evidence that would give some insight, but it's not allowed to be viewed or photographed, according to the gentleman who gave us the tour. According to legend, the spirit of a girl named Johanna still lingers there today.

It is unfortunate when all that is left of a life are the tragic stories and rumors that may or may not be proven through research. During the gaming days of the 1930s and 40s, Johanna was reported to be the daughter of the club owner or one of the managers. Since the owners of the Primrose Club, later known as the Latin Quarter, were Buck Brady and "Red" Masterson, I searched in vain for a Johanna Brady or Masterson. Checking census records of births and deaths, as well as obituaries from both Newport and Cincinnati, I still was unable to unearth evidence of the reported events. It is for certain that a girl named Johanna died there. The events surrounding her death are what are left for conjecture and speculation from the writers and researchers. I will, however, tell the story according to the local legends I have heard and found through research.

Jazz babies, speakeasies, illegal bourbon, showgirls, and organized crime are all things one might have found at Buck Brady's Primrose Club in the 1930s and 1940s. Buck and his associate, Red Masterson, were the owners and operators of the club, which would later reopen as a casino and bingo hall called the Latin Quarter. The Primrose Club was opened by Brady, who refused to let it be run by an organized crime ring based out of Cleveland. He had been doing well on his own and had no need of any "help" from outsiders. However, the pressure was on and he got wind that members of a crime ring known as the "Cleveland Four" and a gentleman by the name of Sam Tucker who represented them and their interest

This is the door to the tiny, unlit room where the dancing girls would keep their children so they could work. The children would be locked in there and forced to stay in the dark for as long as their mother's worked. The doorway and the room are connected to the well room so there is no telling what the children saw in that basement.

in gaining control of the Newport area business were out to get him. He decided to strike first and in August of 1946, he lay in wait for Red Masterson, another affiliate. According to the thorough research of two Eastern Kentucky University students, Matthew DeMechelle and Gary Potter, the story went as follows:

"On August 5, 1946, Brady lay in wait for Masterson outside the Merchant's Club. As Red was getting into his car Brady fired a shotgun (apparently Newport's weapon of choice) at him, wounding but not killing Masterson. During his attempt at escape Brady ran his car into several parked cars and had to flee on foot. The police found Brady hiding in an outhouse and promptly arrested him for disturbing the peace (Messick, 1968; 39-40).

In the spirit of true organized crime camaraderie, Masterson refused to identify Brady as the shooter at his trial, and George

There is a filmy apparition which looks to be the figure of a woman. She appears to have her head so I do not know if this is Pearl, Johanna, or perhaps just a working girl who keeps replaying the nights when she put her children in that room.

Door to the children's room comparative photograph.

Remus showed up as a character witness for Buck. The disturbing the peace charge was quickly dropped. The Cleveland Four saw no reason to prolong the incident with another public act of violence. They told Brady to leave Newport or be killed. Wisely, Brady retired to Florida after giving the Primrose to the Cleveland Four as a peace offering. The Cleveland Four renamed the club the Latin Quarter, remodeled and expanded it. Dave Whitfield, one of the arsonists from the Beverly Hills Club fire was given the job of manager after his release from prison (Messick, 1968: 39-40)."[7]

Some legends would have us believe that the suicide of the girl named Johanna was linked to Brady, Masterson, or another boss who ran the club. However, it seems that she was likely just a showgirl or dancer who worked at the club and finding information about her death is difficult, as no one seems to know her last name. Could it be that Johanna was a stage name, hiding the identity of a young girl who wanted desperately to make it in the big time, but was doing well to sing, dance, or even prostitute herself at the local club? The evidence of prostitution in Wilder, Kentucky is immense, so it's not a far stretch to believe that Johanna was just another girl who, like Pearl Bryan, had a terrible problem and no way out. Perhaps suicide seemed the only option. However, in keeping with legend, the story is told that Johanna was in love with a singer at the club. His name was Robert Randall and it will never be known if he knew that she was pregnant or planned to do anything about it. All that is known is that Johanna was in trouble and keeping secrets such as these is almost impossible in a small town and in a business like the Club. It was not long before Johanna's father found out about the love affair between the two and, very likely, the pregnancy. He, being a high wheeling boss in the Club, knew that something must be done about Robert Randall. Driven to an almost homicidal rage, he had one of his gangster friends murder Robert Randall. Pregnant and beside herself with grief, Johanna reportedly killed her father (the most common belief is that she poisoned him) and then committed suicide herself. I could not verify whether this happened when the site was still known as the Primrose Club, owned by Brady and Masterson, or whether it had already changed hands and had become the Latin Quarter Casino. While I know there must have been a grain of truth planted in the memories of those who remember the incident, the facts have become lost somewhere in the annals of time. I searched death records and obituaries from all over the area attempting to find some evidence that this actually happened. An event as horrific as a murder/suicide usually always makes the papers in some way, if not on the front page. Unfortunately, all I came up with was legends that have been passed down from one generation of ghost hunters and locals to the next. Is the suicide note that is scrawled on the catwalk for real? We may never know for sure. Certainly there are enough people who know the story for there to be at least reasonable speculation that this actually occurred. I just wish I could have found more tangible evidence on the lives and deaths of these people. What is certain is that it makes for very good storytelling at Bobby Mackey's.

Death in the Latin Quarter

I find it frustrating when I am unable to uncover factual accounts of events that everyone knows took place inside this building. One story is about a man whom everyone knows only as "Rodriguez." Rodriguez was a worker in the Latin Quarter. Working late one evening, I suppose no one noticed when he did not come home. The next day, however, he was found dead at the bottom of the basement stairs. I cannot verify what happened to the man. He could have had a heart attack and laid there and died or, since stories have had a tendency to run this way, he could have been pushed by the same force that

If you look off to the left hand side you will note a transparent figure. It looks as if he is crouching down, but the boards that indicate where the stairs used to be are quite visible through the figure. Could this be the worker that died on the stairs and was not found until the next day?

pushed Bobby Mackey's wife Janet. The truth as it was told to me is that they found him dead and that he still haunts that sight. I am including this small but interesting story because when I photographed the stairs, I caught something on my camera that was not there when I shot it. Is it the spirit of Rodriguez, crouched at the bottom where he died? You can be the judge!

Satanic Rituals? Probably not.

As if the accounts of murder and suicide were not enough for this tiny little town in Northern Kentucky, it would appear that a good dose of Satanism is just what the doctor ordered to put this place on the map. Since the site used to be a slaughterhouse in the early 1800s, they did need a place to dump animal remains and to drain the blood and this was

Detail.

done both in the well on the premises and down into the Licking River, located just yards away. Where there is blood, there is always the rumor of Satan worship and the slaughter of innocent young virgins, and Wilder Kentucky is no exception to this. However, the historian in me keeps reminding me that this was the early 1800s! The probability of the performance of Satanic rituals or occult activity is very low, as most people

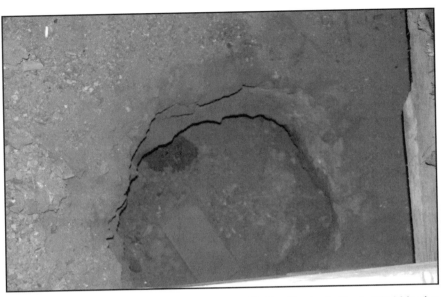

"Hell's Gate Well." The well in the basement of Bobby Mackey's Music World is also known as "Hell's Gate" according to local legend. The reports of Satanic activity are apocryphal as far as I can tell, but what is certain is that local legends certainly fuel the fire!

were scared to death to even be accused of witchcraft, much less anything else. The United States Census report from the years 1800-1840 indicates that the entirety of Campbell County, which is where Bobby Mackey's was located, had a maximum of about 5,000 people living in the vicinity. This was spread out over a three hundred mile radius. The likelihood of any satanic ritual occurring without every neighbor knowing about it and throwing a good old fashioned, God fearing, Bible belt hissy fit would strain credulity, indeed.

The Possession of Carl Lawson

Because of the hype surrounding Carl Lawson and his demonic possession, I would be remiss to exclude it. Many of the details we have about the basement of Bobby Mackey's and the stories of the strange happenings that go on in there are attributable to Carl Lawson. Lawson was hired by Bobby as a handyman and general worker when he first purchased the building. Carl was a decent man who lived by himself and kept much of what he began to witness in the building to himself. The story is told that Carl began to experience strange things after everyone left at night. The jukebox would turn on by itself, even though it was unplugged, and play the "Anniversary Waltz!" The smell of roses would be thick in the air and that was, according to Carl, how he knew that the spirit – later identified as "Johanna" – was present. She had a signature rose scented perfume that other bar workers testified smelling. Carl reported seeing strange, angry men in the bar area — men who were obviously ghosts. The strangeness did not end there as he was finally able to speak to these entities, holding conversations with them, and eventually being possessed by spirits. According to Tyler Lucas, a long time patron of the bar and local man whose family has lived in the area of Southgate for as long as he can remember, Carl had a dream one night about the murder of Pearl Bryan. He said that Carl saw everything in great detail and had been visited by the spirits of Pearl, Scott, and Alonzo. He had seen everything; the murder, the concealment of the head, and the hanging. He was so greatly moved and upset by the dream that he went down to the basement and immediately began tearing up the floor, thereby discovering the remains of the old well where Pearl's head supposedly rests still today. It is obvious from the condition of the floor that the well had been built over and, most likely forgotten, except by those who remember the story of Pearl Bryan's murder. Carl had torn up the floor, hacking away at it until it revealed the location of the well – just as he had witnessed in his dream. When I visited, it was still as it had been that night – intact in most all the area except for where the well, a sunken hole dug straight into the ground, sat. Carl maintained that the spirits had revealed it to him and that he was certain he had been possessed. As the building was undergoing renovations at the time, the strange events and happenings at the bar had increased. As it was explained to me, when buildings are renovated, often the spirits that linger there become agitated and angry. Just like human beings, when our environment changes and strangers come in to change places that we know and are familiar with, it often leads to irritability and discomfort. Supposedly, the same thing happens with disembodied spirits. They do not appreciate change, even change for the better. Often, they will continue to pass through the same wall, where there once stood a doorway when they knew the place. The will walk the same paths they knew in life, even though new structures are there. For Carl, the strange possession did not stop there—the renovations only increased its frequency and intensity. He sprinkled holy water over the well, hoping to quell the discontent of the spirits, but only infuriated them further and causing them to wreak more havoc, now bordering on poltergeist activity. He claims to have been violently pushed, a complaint that Janet Mackey would also make at a later date. The stairs that led to the basement — the same stairs on which Rodriguez died — were becoming more dangerous, it would seem. Janet was walking down the stairs when she was picked up around the waist and then the force violently attempted to push her down the stairs. At the same time, she heard a voice saying "Get out!" coming from the top of the stairs. She was five months pregnant at the time. Interestingly, she was as far along in her pregnancy as both Johanna and Pearl Bryan were at the time of their deaths. Coincidence? Perhaps. Carl continued to have visions and finally had to employ the services of a local priest who performed an exorcism and finally rid Carl of the spirits who haunted him.

The Night I Visited

After doing intensive research and finding myself more and more intrigued with every story I would hear, I could not wait to make the two hour drive to Wilder, Kentucky. It was February 29, 2008. Not knowing how to get there and not quite sure what I would find when I arrived, I took along my trusty husband and best supporter, Jim. While neither of us would be much of a match for anyone wanting to brawl, he did feel that going into a strange, reportedly haunted bar by myself would be folly. So we drove and drove, letting our faculties of internal navigation lead the way, and enjoying the time we had to spend together. Something told me that this night was going to be a very interesting one, though, when our route was diverted about an hour outside of Wilder. Traffic was backed up on I71 North and we were directed off the expressway and onto an old country road that made me certain I was going to see a little boy playing "Dueling Banjos" at any given moment. It was dark, deserted, and it wasn't until we pulled off to ask for directions that we found out that just a mile up the road from where we were detoured, there was a terrible accident involving a semi-truck. There had been at least one fatality. I became a little nauseated at that point, realizing that my entire purpose behind this trip was motivated by death — and here it was, as if to meet me along my way, not one mile in front of me. I considered turning back around and going home at that point, wondering if the expressway fatality was a bad omen; I shook that off, letting my logic and reason take over and telling myself that there were no such things as ghosts and bad omens, just unfortunate circumstances. In retrospect, I think that is what we tell ourselves in order to be able to get through our own fears of what really might be lurking in realms we do not understand. For the moment, though, I convinced myself and continued on my way to the bar. Stopping along the way for bottled water, I asked some of the locals about their experiences there. Most agreed that strange things frequent there with the regularity and with as much predictability as the locals who make it their weekly hang out. Almost all had their own experiences, ranging from chairs that were knocked over by themselves, doors that open and close without anyone being around, and fans that spin one rotation and then stop when noticed. Almost all accept the spirited events as normal and would not stop visiting the establishment over something so small as a haunting.

When we arrived at Bobby Mackey's Jim and I stood outside the building, noting that it looked more like a rundown warehouse than a bar, but only stayed a moment due to the fiercely cold wind that blew through us. It was the kind of biting cold that comes only from a breeze off of a river, and I wondered how cold Pearl must have been on the night she was brought into Fort Thomas. We went in and I was amazed at the darkness of the interior and the fact that they are a cash only bar. We had to turn around and hit the only ATM in town, located at a local dairy mart. Coming back armed with a notebook, camera, and cash in hand, we were then ready to begin to trek into the unknown. I felt oddly out of place, as the rest of the patrons obviously knew that I was neither local, nor interested in riding the large mechanical bull located off to the right of the bar area. I wanted to just sit and talk to people, but that can often be misconstrued as inviting behavior and I opted to speak to Bobby first and just let him know who I was and why I was there. Having obtained permission from the bar manager, Donna, I thought it wise to make Bobby privy to my endeavor and he was a most accommodating gentleman. His curly grey hair and blue jean jacket gave no indication that he was anyone other than another patron, but I recognized him from his pictures. He warmly greeted me and we chatted about the place and its history. We laughed about misconceptions that people had and he was more than kind about my presence there. I found him to be one of the nicest people I had encountered and I parted from him with promises that I would not disturb any of the patrons.

I was unsure where to start, but Bobby had directed me to a person whom he said had stories about the happenings in the bar and was a frequent visitor. The tall, dark haired man couldn't have been over thirty and I felt a little shy about questioning him since he was there to have a good time and not be bothered. He identified himself as Matt Coates and said that he saw ghosts there all the time. He said that he saw shadows walking around the bar when there was no one else around and that figures would walk among the people as if they were there having a good time, too. He was reticent to give many details and I decided that it would be best to let him continue his down time and move on to others.

It didn't take long for people to start seeking me out and giving me their stories of strange happenings, as well. Tyler Lucas said that they used to have a fortuneteller who set up shop in the tiny hallway between the pool tables and the mechanical bull pit. He said that strange things would happen there, things such as chairs that were stacked on top of the tables knocking over by themselves. He was a plethora of information and extremely easy-going. His casual manner immediately put me at ease and it was from him that I learned much of the oral history of the building. After speaking with him for a while, I realized that I couldn't put off the journey to the basement much longer. However, I realized that I had been hesitant to go there, even though I had already purchased a ticket for the tour. The entire trip revolved around the basement and the head still hidden in its depths and so I made my way through the bodies I could see to hopefully capture pictures of the ones I couldn't.

The notorious basement stairs have long since been torn down and never rebuilt, so our guide led us out the front doors and around the side of the building to a side door that led to the basement area. I tried hard not to feel a little sick, since I realized that I was entering an area that, if rumor was correct, had been filled with death since its very first days. When I walked through the large wooden door, the first thing that struck me was the smell. I know that logically there could be no remnants of the slaughterhouse left after more than one hundred years, but the stench was so strong that it literally hit me full it in the face. It was a smell I can't even describe and yet I don't want it to appear that I was sensing anything "other-worldly." It was a very real smell, like the stench of rotting meat. The first item that caught my eye, however, was not the infamous well, but the statue of Jesus standing on a little table as you walk in the door. Dusty, as if left there over a century ago, it really added to the feeling that we were walking into a place where He would need to be. Our guide, Eric, let us meander around as we wished, but of course I really wanted to see the well. It was off in a little room, pretty much by itself. A board railing was put up around it, I suppose so that no one would get the urge to start digging into it any more than they had. There were broken plates around and I could see where Carl Lawson himself had torn up the floor in order to find the well. What I hadn't been told about, and what held interest for me, however, was the little room that was directly behind the well. It was dark and small, too small for anything but maybe a closet, and damp—you could see the exposed brick and feel the coldness from within. Not a ghost story, but a horror story went along with that room. It was where the dancers and showgirls, and likely the prostitutes would lock their children while they worked. I could only imagine the cries that must still be locked inside the walls of that room. The inhumanity contained within those walls was as strong as the miasmic stench of sewage and death that followed us wherever we went. I tried for one moment to imagine myself in the shoes of one of the girls. Alone, trying to make ends meet by dancing for drunks and slobbering old men, she would have had to put her children somewhere. What if there was no sitter, no family? How would she pay the rent? Eat? The girls who locked their little one away inside that damp, dark room surely must have died a little inside every time they shut the door. And, I also began to wonder what the children saw when they were down there, alone and in the dark? I did not see anything while I was there. There was another couple who was touring the basement with us and they had brought their EVP with them. I was a little glad that they did because in the picture that I captured something was at that moment the machine went crazy. I cannot verify what the readings were, because, quite honestly, I am not educated in that area and would not know a good reading from a bad one. However, what I can say is that at the moment I heard them say that the machine was going crazy, I pointed my camera in the direction they were monitoring and snapped a picture. Just a few seconds after I took the shot, their machine died. There was absolutely no battery charge at all. Interestingly, I had watched the man put in new batteries just five minutes before. While I would not speculate about what they were monitoring or what they caught, what I can produce is what I caught on film at that moment. I suppose there is something to be said for being in the right place at the right time!

Is Bobby Mackey's haunted? I think without a doubt there is evidence to suggest that something other than drunks and local patrons haunt this place on a regular basis. While I did not see anything firsthand, I did capture a few pictures that would make me stop and take a second look if I were a serious ghost hunter looking for some really good evidence. The people are friendly and Bobby Mackey is accommodating to all who enter. So the next time you are crossing from Ohio into Kentucky, you might want to stop at this little out-of-the-way country and western bar. While you might not have a run-in with the headless body of Pearl Bryan's ghost, there is a very good chance that you will meet people who can tell you stories that one day you can tell your grandchildren and great-grandchildren. And, oh, by the way — I would not suggest stopping in if you are pregnant, the regulars there who never leave seem to be bothered by that. Plus, if you catch a strong whiff of a rose scented perfume, don't turn around. Just put a coin in the jukebox and have a dance to the Anniversary Waltz in memory of Johanna.

Spring Street Bar and Grill

S pring Street Bar and Grill, located at 300 South Spring Street in Louisville, is a place with which I am very familiar, since many of the evenings of my mis-spent youth ended up there for a scrumptious bite to eat after a long night of music and merriment. In all the time I spent there, I never had any idea that Spring Street carried with it the reputation of being a famous haunted location. I was only aware that they were famous for serving their patrons the very best onion rings found in the east

Jockey silks remind patrons of our Derby heritage and add nice ambiance to the bar area.

end of the city; I had no idea that a much more interesting claim to fame was lurking right beneath my feet and just over my head.

The History

The site of the old National Bar might not be listed on the Historic Register, either nationally or locally, but that does not mean that its importance to the history of the community is diminished. While I could not find an immense amount of information on the history of the building, what I do know is like many of the local taverns, it pre-dates prohibition and is remembered as having quite the reputation in its heyday. When I spoke with former employee Elly Flaherty, she gave me some of the history of the building that has been passed down through the years. Her thirteen years with the establishment allowed her to get to know many of the long time customers and neighborhood locals, who would pass along information to her. It might not surprise anyone to know that the bar and grill was a former Speakeasy and that the door that leads to the basement could only be accessed by using a specific knock, rapped out a specific number of times. Once inside, the liquor and bathtub gin flowed, the musicians played, and the girls of the evening scouted the place for their next trick. The walls were painted with scenes of dancing girls and musical notes, which still exist almost one hundred years later. The paint is peeling and the guts of a long abandoned piano stand alone in the back corner. The basement is damp and I can only imagine that back in the day, this must have been the hot spot of the city.

The basement was not the only place that would be jumping when the patrons came to call, however. The stairs that wind up to the third floor provided access for the local prostitutes to take their Johns upstairs to a fully functioning brothel. The long corridor is still lined with doors that once had numbers on them and girls inside who were waiting for company and cash. While there were no murders or strange incidents that happened at the brothel, one can only imagine that the girls who spent so much

In the basement of the bar you can still see the paintings of the dancing girls, martini glasses, and musical notes along the wall. These are still exactly as they were when they were painted so very long ago.

time and gave so much of themselves must have left some sort of residual energy there long after they were gone. The numbers are gone from the doors and the rooms are no longer rocking with the sounds of energetic lovers, but some say that the girls are not really ever gone.

The Girls Who Stay

From what I gather, there are two types of spirit energy, *residual and intelligent*. I am certainly not an expert on differentiating the two kinds, as I rarely hang around long enough to get any information. Ever the chicken hearted one, I can only surmise that what the employees and patrons experience is some type of residual energy that stays due to the amount of energy that was expended in the rooms and down below. I do not discount nor deny that there could be "intelligence" haunting this bar and grill, but most of what the long time workers tell me is that hearing strange sounds is the most common occurrence. Elly explained that for the longest time, she refused to go upstairs to the office area (formerly the house of ill repute) by herself. She would be working by herself, sometimes cleaning up or closing down for the night. In the dead silence, she would hear bracelets clinking down the hallway. She explained that it sounded like a thin, tinkling sound and it made her hearken back to the days when women would wear several tiny bracelets on one arm. It was definitely the sound of a lady, Elly explained, and this was reinforced even further when she began hearing the sounds of footsteps. I told her that some people had reported seeing a man, but she immediately told me that the footsteps were definitely that of a woman. She went on to explain that they were not the heavy, tramping feet of a man wearing heavy shoes, but the light steps of a lady, which make a very distinct sound. She said that they sounded like high heels on the wooden floors above and were quick and deliberate. Shortly after, the door would slam.

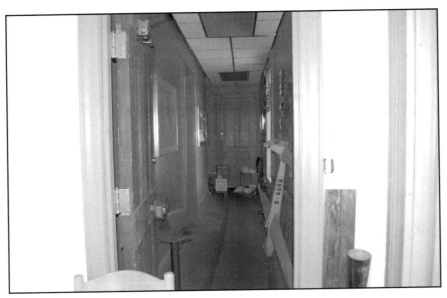

The hallway of ill repute. This is where the ladies would lead their men for an evening of pleasure. It remains pretty much the same and this is where most of the activity occurs when the lights are out even today.

Slamming doors were not unusual occurrences in the building. Many of the workers, including a gentleman named Tim, who was kind enough to give me the tour, have reported being alone and hearing doors slam shut — even when there is no obvious breeze or cross current to be found. Could the sound be someone who is angry letting the people who occupy the place now know that they are still here after all these years? Perhaps, like most of us, the spirits who remain simply do not want to be forgotten. Could the sound of the bracelets and high heels be the spirit of some long forgotten madam retracing the steps that she walked so many times during her life? When people do things repetitively throughout a number of years, maybe they continue to do that in the afterlife, as well. Whatever the reason or the cause, Spring Street Bar and Grill has convinced all who work there and many who do not that there is most definitely an "other-worldly" presence that continues to make itself known.

These are the stairs that lead to the neon graveyard in the attic. I included this shot because I was not standing anywhere that I could cast a shadow and there was no one else near the area. This shadow appears to be pointing up the stairs, but I'm not confident enough to say with certainty that it's a shadow person. In comparative shots, there was nothing there and no other shadows turned up.

These stairs lead to nowhere. They are located in the basement, but I did not see at first what I did see later, which was the shadow figure of a man in a fedora style hat. He is off to the right of the stairs.

8

Octagon Hall

S ometimes a house will catch a person's eye because of the beauty of the architecture or the intricacy of the design. When I first saw the home of Andrew Jackson Caldwell on the web, I was immediately intrigued because I had never seen an octagonal shaped home before. It was lovely in its individualistic simplicity, but I did not know at the time that the story that it held inside its strangely shaped walls was really one of sorrow, death, and the vicious unrest that lives in the closet upstairs. I was to spend an immense amount of time in what is now known as Octagon Hall and by the end of my visit, if I never believed that anything was left after our bodies departed this realm of consciousness, I certainly did after that experience.

I am re-printing the history of this beautiful antebellum home and museum with the kind permission of its current owners, Billy and Barry Byrd. These brothers invited me to come visit their establishment and greeted me with all the grace, charm, and hospitality of refined Southern gentlemen.

The History

This excerpt is taken from the brochure given to me by Billy Byrd and is re-printed with his kind permission.

In 1847, Andrew Jackson Caldwell laid the first foundation stone for a house unlike any in the region. Using handmade bricks from local soil and timbers from his woods, he completed his task in 1859 and Octagon Hall was born. A local landmark, the Hall has endured to become the only surviving octagonal house in Kentucky. Natural limestone blocks weighing up to 1 ½ tons provide the support for the massive brick structure. Completed before the onset of hostilities between the states, Octagon Hall was to become a strategic asset to both Confederate and Union forces. Located on the L&N Railroad and the Nashville Pike, it was ideally suited for an observation post and camp area. With enemy forces advancing from the front and left flank, the Confederate Army at Bowling Green, Kentucky evacuated the city and forts. On February 13, 1862, approximately 8,000 Confederates and Commanders camped at Octagon Hall on their march to Tennessee. Union forces occupied the area days later, killing the family cattle and poisoning the drinking water from the well with the carcasses they threw there. The Hall was used as a hiding place for CSA (Confederate States of America) troops throughout the war.

On the grounds of Octagon Hall, you will find a slave quarters, intact in hand hewn timbers, a slave cemetery, summer kitchen, which is located away from the house, and the largest dogwood tree in Kentucky.

Octagon Hall has undergone few structural changes. Dr. Mike Williams, the 2nd owner, removed the cupola due to fire damage in 1918. This cupola was used to hide Confederate soldiers and valuables during the Civil War. The Caldwells placed the Confederate soldiers they were hiding from the Union forces in the cupola. There were beehives in the cupola, so the Caldwell family would dress the hidden soldiers in bee keeper's suits and deterring the Union troops from investigating further as they did not want to be stung.

Octagon Hall as see from the back near the slave quarters.

Why An Octagon?

Architecture often reveals much about the time period, culture, and fads or fashions of the time in which a building was constructed. Octagonal or eight-sided homes were no exception to this. During the mid-nineteenth century, approximately 1,850–1,860, people were fascinated with things that were unusual or considered exotic. There were at least 1,000 — some estimate closer to 2,000 — octagon houses constructed in the United States during this time period and of those numbers, only about six hundred remain standing. Many of the pictures I saw showed homes in disrepair that were being renovated for modern families. The octagon shaped home was inspired by architect and noted phrenologist of the time, Orson Squire Fowler. Fowler wrote two books on the subject of octagon houses and their connection to better overall health. He stated that they provided more air and sunlight than a regular four sided or traditionally built home. The cupola on the top, which was, I am assuming, supposed to be mandatory for this style home, would bring in better sunlight and allow better airflow throughout the home. According to some people I have interviewed, this is not a far-fetched idea. When the windows in a well constructed cupola are opened and the windows on the lower levels of the home are opened, it provides a current that does circulate up and out of the cupola, possibly with the expectation that the "bad air" and germs would travel up and out of the home. While it might seem faddish, the octagon house is unique and did make quite the statement about the owners, visually expressing their expectation of finer and more aesthetically pleasing surroundings.

The Caldwell Family and the War Between the States

Technically, Kentucky remained a neutral state during the Civil War, but most would agree that this is true only on paper. While the war divided an entire nation, Kentucky was also split in two, with those in the northern portion of the state remaining true to the Union and its ideas of abolition and the unity of the states. However, the southern portion of the state housed families who had large farms and plantations and did not want the Union telling them what they could do with what they viewed as their "property." Kentucky was, in fact, a neutral state that would not take sides against the Union, but was still considered a slave state at the time. Therefore, families who had large land holdings, like the Caldwells, were southern sympathizers. Simpson County is located very near the Tennessee border and its ties to southern traditions and beliefs about the rights of property holders made it an area where loyalties to the CSA could easily be discerned just by looking at the properties around.

Andrew Jackson Caldwell and Elizabeth Akers Caldwell were married in 1844, three years before construction of Octagon Hall began. Their eldest daughter, Frances Ellen, was born in January of 1845. She alone was the surviving child of this union, as both Elizabeth and an unnamed infant son died in 1851: Elizabeth on June 9 and her son on November 8. I wondered if there were lingering effects of the birth that might have caused her death. The infant was born on April 22 and she died not even two months later. This would indicate to me that there might have been post-partum complications that continued to worsen until they resulted in her death. Infection or unchecked gestational hypertension would be likely causes, but no one can be sure. After all, there were no neo-natal units and no way to make sure that the mother and child were indeed well after the birth. These were not the only tragedies to occur in Octagon Hall, but rather the beginning of a long list of deaths, illnesses, and tragedies brought about by war or bad luck. The most tragic death reported would have to be that of the little daughter that Elizabeth and Andrew named Mary Elizabeth. She was born on July 14, 1847, the year that construction began on Octagon Hall. She died at the age of seven, on September 1, 1854, three years after the death of her mother. In those days, little girls wore long dresses and lacy or frilly little pantaloons that showed beneath their skirts. I can only imagine her bouncing and flouncing around the house in her little outfits, being precocious as only charming little girls can. However, for some inexplicable reason she was in the winter kitchen that fateful September day. She went too near to the fireplace that day, either poking into it with a stick or a poker, as the story goes, and her little dress caught fire. She burned to death, her family unable to help her in any way. That kind of tragedy marks a family forever, and even though her mother was already deceased, it must have been a severe blow to the rest of the household. Most families had many children for several reasons, the most obvious being that birth control was not a common practice and the less obvious being that half of all children were expected to die during infancy and childhood due to the fact that common childhood illnesses such as measles, mumps, whooping cough, or scarlet fever had not been eradicated. Additionally, there were no antibiotics to treat infections or pneumonia and if a child developed an intestinal disorder such as diarrhea, they would simply dehydrate and die because there was no such thing as an IV or saline drip. Mothers and fathers knew that it was common to lose children at a young age, but to lose a child to such a horrendous tragedy was not a common occurrence. There are no records of how long Mary Elizabeth burned before someone found her or was able to help her or even if she was alone in the kitchen that day, but the burns must have been so severe that she would have been nearly unrecognizable to those who loved her. She was buried behind the house where her mother and infant brother were laid to rest just a few short years before.

Just speculating on the event itself, I am left to wonder about why Mary Elizabeth was left alone that day. Andrew Jackson Caldwell had not remarried at that time. He would not remarry until a year later when he took Harriet Morton to be his wife. Could it be that it was simply a mistake and the child who was left without a mother to look after her was following around one of the slaves who worked in the kitchen? Maybe there was a "Mammy" figure that stepped in at the death of Mary Elizabeth's mother and took over the care-giving of the two little motherless girls. That would explain why she would have been in the kitchen that day, perhaps tagging along behind and trying to be helpful. In my mind, this tragic accident was nothing more than childish bad judgment and the longing desire to be near to a mother figure that felt as warm and familiar as the food cooking in the winter kitchen that day. It could have been that she was not poking around, but truly trying to help whoever was in the kitchen that day. Perhaps she was stirring the pot, hoping to make someone proud of the way she was able to be a big girl. Maybe she was helping stoke or poke at the fire in order to make it hotter so that dinner would be ready on time. Perhaps, the person in the kitchen expected her to help out around the house and had told her to go put something in the fire and could not tell anyone that it was she who had caused the tragedy. There are many different explanations for what might have happened, but no matter what the real circumstance, it would appear that Mary Elizabeth never really left the home to which she was so attached.

Andrew went on to marry Harriet Morton on Christmas night, December 25, 1855. Together they had several children together, including one set of twins. One child, Emily, died at the age of two in 1862 and in 1866, the year that Harriet was pregnant with their last child, Virginia Nichol, Andrew Jackson Caldwell, Sr. died of typhoid fever.

Who Haunts Octagon Hall?

While I am certain that Octagon Hall saw its share of happiness, one has to wonder about the lingering effects of such an immense amount of tragedy and pain. Not only were there many deaths of the occupants of the home, the wounded and dying soldiers that would sometimes appear on the doorstep of Octagon Hall must have left some sort of residual mark on the building itself. There were at least two documented cases of wounded Confederate soldiers who came to the home to be treated and died there. One soldier came to the door with a severe wound to his leg and foot. The household members were unable to treat him properly as the Union soldiers could be heard coming right behind him. They took the young man up the stairs to the attic room that led to the cupola, a favorite place for stashing soldiers on the run from the Yankees. They had to wait overnight before it was safe enough to go check on the young man in the attic. When they found him, the sight was worse than what they had expected. Unable to get help for the wound in his leg, he was laying dead in a pool of his own blood. He had bled to death overnight. His body was never identified and therefore no family or friends were ever notified of his whereabouts or what happened to him. There was no way to identify him and so the family took him out behind the house and buried him in a grave that was marked "CSA Unknown Soldier" with his date of death. This would be the fate of another young man who showed up at the Caldwell home. Wounded beyond help, he must have shown up in the middle of the night, unable to call for help or so close to death that it did not matter. When the family arose the next morning, they found him dead on their front doorstep. He died there during the night and was later buried in the same type of grave and next to the other Unknown Soldier. There are grave markers showing where the two rest, but sadly, there is no way that their families would ever know where they are.

Are these the only soldiers that stick around the last place that they knew on earth? Probably not. It has been speculated that there are many spirits who linger on, roaming the grounds of Octagon Hall, some reports listing their numbers in the thousands. At least two slaves, Ben and Henry, have been reported walking the grounds and one little slave girl has been captured on EVP, according to Billy Byrd. After I heard the EVP myself, I did not doubt it. They have captured what appears to be the voice of Mary Elizabeth calling for her "Mommy" and at least one southern soldier in a deep Mississippi drawl calling someone a "Dumb Ass." While I could not believe what I was hearing, there was no denying what it said! I wondered to myself if that voice was in some way connected to the buttons that Billy found in the hiding place under the front stairs. It seems that there was yet another hiding place constructed that had been dug out under the front stairs. It is no bigger than a crawl space, but two men could lie side by side in it and when the doors were closed, they would likely go undetected by Union troops. In that crawl space Billy found CSA buttons, one with the name of a Mississippi unit on it.

Perhaps, the man on the EVP was none other than the man who must have hidden under those stairs. A more menacing spirit who is reported to haunt the antebellum museum lingers in the closet and the attic space that used to lead to the burned out cupola. Most of the people who have dared to climb the treacherous angle and crawl through the space to get to the attic have not been disappointed in what they have found—although most have been truly frightened. One gentleman reported that while on a supernatural investigation at Octagon Hall a few months before, he braved the attic and "saw what he needed to see." Not at all the type of person to be shaken by restless spirits, this gentleman was also extremely calm and level headed. I asked him about his experience and this was what he reported:

> He had been investigating Octagon Hall and the unexplained activities therein. He crawled up into the attic and before he could even settle in and turn on his equipment, he came face-to-face with what appeared to be a man in a Confederate uniform.
>
> "It was like watching a horror movie," he said. "He was laying on his side and there was blood everywhere. It was coming from his leg and he was in a lot of pain. There was just blood everywhere."

He left the attic shortly after that, stating, "that was it." No further proof was needed to make him a believer that there is definitely something lingering in Octagon Hall. What is interesting is that what he saw directly coincided with the story of the Confederate soldier who bled to death in the attic. Could this have been the same man, reliving his last few moments on earth? Is he trapped and angry? It appears to be so due to the malevolent nature of the spirit who has been seen in that area. While not necessarily violent, witnesses state that there is just something "dark" about it and that they get a very negative feeling from that particular place in the house.

The Investigation

Middle Tennessee Ghost Chasers (MTGC)

I wasn't prepared for what I walked into when I went to Octagon Hall that day. I had my mind set to the fact that I would go, take some pictures, do an interview or two, and then head back home. Running into a full-blown ghost investigation was not what I had planned on for my evening. When I pulled into the parking lot, Billy and his two brothers met me. According to my watch, I pulled in around 5:00, which is their closing time. Fortunately, because I am on Eastern Standard Time and they are on Central, it was only 4:00 their time. I thought I only had a few minutes, when, in fact, I had almost an hour. We all sat and talked, looked at pictures on their website, and listened to EVP's. It was almost 5:00 by the time I finally made it into the house itself, and Billy made his apologies that he would not be able to stay much longer. He explained that there would be an investigative team arriving any moment and that he was not certain that they would allow me to stay. However, if they did give me permission I was welcome to follow along behind them. It was an opportunity that was once in a lifetime for me.

As I walked through the house alone, I waited for the team to arrive. I did not have to wait long. I had taken about three hundred pictures, two of which I was anxious to see up close, when the team arrived. I was not sure what I had been prepared to see, perhaps thinking that I would be face-to-face with the little lady from "Poltergeist," clamoring out of the car screaming, "Stay away from the light, Carol Ann! Don't go into the light!" But, it was nothing like that at all. The team, comprised mostly of couples, husbands and wives, was as normal as anyone you would meet off the street. They were nurses and computer guys, all who take a very keen interest in finding proof of life after death. They were

This was the first picture taken at Octagon Hall and Billy snickered when I showed it to him, astonished and excited that I had captured a picture of something. He was very familiar with the lurking, dark shadow that hangs around these stairs and has many like this on his website.

129

not pseudo would-be-psychic nut jobs that came rolling out of a VW Bus in a cloud of smoke. They came in as anyone would, in regular cars, with regular lives. To be honest, it was reassuring and comforting to know that they were really, just like me, people who took a keen interest in things that were mysterious and difficult to explain.

I introduced myself and set about explaining what I was doing there, and then casually invited myself along on their expedition. I promised I would not get in the way, nor be a burden to anyone, hoping that this would ease any fears about my jeopardizing their investigation. They were more than gracious, telling me I could report or take pictures of anyone or anything they did. They were totally open and honest about the entire investigation, their only hope being that they would capture more proof and "see what they came to see." To be honest, I was hoping the same thing. I knew that I had some interesting pictures, but I was still waiting for "the one." It's the picture that we all hope to get—the one that definitively takes any doubt away that there is something that exists after we cease to. I hoped that with their help I would get that picture that night.

As the darkness began to fall, I met up with two members of the team that were close to my age, Dana and LeeAnn. We stood around, talking and giggling, and I found it interesting that similar personality types will always gravitate toward each other. We chit chatted as the twilight gave way to dusk and we made our way out to the slave cemetery, where two of the more sensitive members of the team were feeling their way around. They both stopped at the grave of a man they identified as "Henry." They could feel him and his spirit and could both hear him talking to them. They knelt down in the middle of the grove of trees where the slaves were buried. The trees had grown into a circle, surrounding the bodies with shade and protecting the small, chipped stones from further erosion. As they knelt there at the gravesite of Henry, they were both overcome with emotion. The one man, whom they called Bruiser because of his enormous size and strength, could *feel* Henry and all of the injustice, sadness, and despair. As this giant of a man knelt at the stone, the greatness of his compassion for his fellow man was apparent. Interestingly, while some may pooh-pooh this kind of experience, it's interesting to note that he picked up on a hand injury that Henry had, an injury that kept him out of the field and close to the house. This, along with a facial injury that they also felt while out at his grave, were both corroborated as actual events that had happened. There had been a slave named Henry, who had injured his hand. They kept him in the house and it appears that he cobbled, or made shoes, for the family. Additionally, the mouth injury, although no one is certain how it happened, was also factual. Those kind of specific descriptions make it a little more difficult to completely dismiss the gifts of the sentient people of the team.

It was not long before the group moved itself inside to get set up for the night. They informed me that, for some reason, nighttime is a much more active time for spirits. I had previously wondered whether or not spirits, if they existed at all, were affected by external conditions. Could they detect light and dark without eyes? Could they feel cold and rain without skin or nerves? Were they able to hear and speak back even though they did not exist in the same time and space as we, the living, did? IF it were possible for them to feel the same things, perhaps they could be affected by those external conditions. The only problem was, of course, that no one could have enough of a conversation with a spirit to ask him or her all these pertinent questions. We could only speculate. Some of the EVPs that Billy had captured actually had given some evidence of spirits being able to detect differences in their environment. One recording had a spirit saying, "Be quiet. They see us." Another EVP had a little girl saying, "I want Mommy." One of the best ones that I heard, which is also on the Octagon Hall website, was the voice of what appeared to be a young slave girl. It said quite plainly, "I ain't carryin' nothin' down for that bitch." All the EVPs that Billy played for me were plain and the voices were unmistakably different, so it could not be that they had been compromised by outside voices. It was truly amazing. I was not able to get any information that night about whether or not the investigative team from MTGC had caught anything on EVP, but later I spoke to one of the team leaders, Tim. He told me that he caught a very plain EVP from one of the rooms where a recorder had been set up. No one else was around in the house and the only people within a reasonable distance from the room were asleep upstairs. He verified that by viewing them on camera. The voice on the EVP said, "Why don't you go to bed?" It was a child's voice, presumably that of Mary Elizabeth. It was caught at a time where everyone was tired and some were actually asleep. Interestingly, one of the strange happenings that occur frequently is that Billy and his brothers will make up the beds, which are large feather beds. They will walk away and do something else, only to return to find large imprints of a person's body on the beds. They will make it up again and walk away, shaking their heads in disbelief. A short time later, they will find the same thing again. It is the imprint of a person's body and it even extends to the pillow on which they would have laid their head. I might not have believed this myself if it weren't for the fact that the day that I went in, Billy had shown me the bed that had just been made up. There was no doubt that the imprint on the bed was that of a full-length body. There was an indentation on the pillow where someone had put their head. However, no one had been in there since it had been made.

Around 8 p.m., the group from MTGC started walking around the grounds. Taking their time, they collected data from each point and then met back at the house. The set up for the group was incredible. There were monitors in almost every room, as well as the personal equipment that each of the investigators carried. Well prepared to document their findings, this group really used a "debunking" method during their investigation. They were looking for hard evidence and there were many things that could be explained away. It was their position that they were looking for the evidence that could withstand scrutiny, making them in

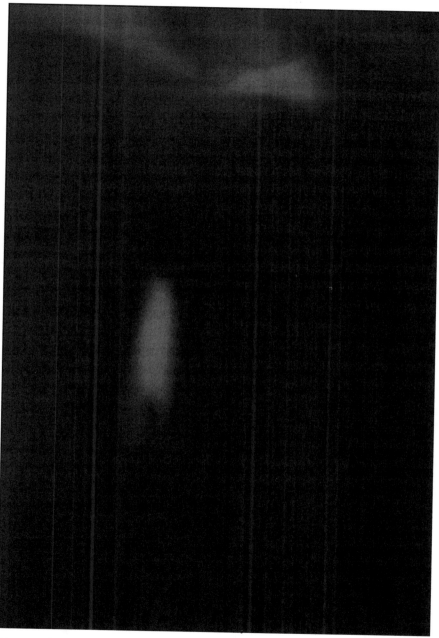

I have no idea what the light at the top of this room is. This was shot into pitch black darkness. The lower light might be a reflection of a bracelet I was wearing, but the top light is completely unrelated to that.

my opinion, a very smart group. In addition to investigating this building, the group was also filming a documentary. It focused on the members and their individual strengths or gifts, as well as the documented findings from sites they investigated previously. It was during this filming that I had my own personal run-in with whatever was inside the house. If I was skeptical in the beginning of this book, one thing is for certain—I cannot explain the things that my camera caught and I cannot explain what happened that night. However, I want to focus on the actual investigation of the team before I report my own experiences, and the team was ready to do work that night. Splitting into groups of three or four, I shadowed the group with Dana, Tina, and Leslie. Beginning in the basement where Mary Elizabeth caught fire, we sat there for about thirty minutes in the dark. Only the light from the meters illuminated the room and to say that it was a little frightening would be an understatement. The women called out to anyone who would respond, but unfortunately, the meters did not reflect any activity and the EVP did not pick up any voices. We moved from room to room doing the same thing, but no hard physical evidence was detected. There was no slamming of doors or shadowy figures that emerged from the darkness. There was only silence and stillness in great, hollow rooms. To make matters worse, it was around midnight when a tornado blew through the area. The trees were whipping around and the lightning was terrible. We took cover in the basement, in the room where Mary Elizabeth died. Amidst the terrible wind and rain, there was the ever present fear that the storm would stir something up that we were not prepared to see and while the rest of the group did not fear this, I did. After hovering there for quite awhile, the storm subsided and we dispersed again to gather back in the central meeting room where the equipment was set up. When I left the investigation at 2 a.m., I had not really seen anything, but I knew without a doubt that there was something there. From my own experience, I was convinced that this was without a doubt one of the most active locations that I had been privileged to see and photograph.

My Own Personal Experience

Coming in as a little more than a storyteller and skeptic, I was not prepared for what happened that evening. When I first went through the building, Billy acted as my guide and gave me the tour. The museum is exceptional, with many original Civil War artifacts resting under glass and I took my time looking at them. However, the first picture I took in Octagon Hall was down the stairs that led to the basement. I was astonished. When I showed the picture to Billy, he laughed as said, "Yeah, it looks like you got our guy." It was a heavy, dark shadow that usually appears on those steps. He was completely familiar with it, but I was not. Even when a person sees something first hand, there is still disbelief about what they are witnessing. I took several comparison shots of the same stairway and none of the others could reproduce the shadowy figure that occurred that was first caught.

Excited by my first "anomaly," I trekked around the house, following behind Billy. He showed me every room and told me the stories that I have recounted here. The eeriest aspect of the tour were the mannequins that were dressed in period style clothes and were present in every room. The soldier stood like a sentinel at the window and the slaves attended a hurt soldier in the "Sick Room." From room to room you cannot walk in without being startled at the figures staring back at you. During the investigation, we laughed about the figures and how creepy they made us feel. By the end of the night, I was afraid that one of those mannequins would move and that I would either freeze in fear and not be able to move, or run away so fast that I would leave my own equipment behind. That, fortunately, did not happen. I walked around with Billy and then asked his permission to go around on my own. I called out to Mary Elizabeth, but I heard nothing in return. I called to the soldier up in the attic and was able to photograph some kind of shadow lurking there. However, I would not be able to say whether or not it was simply just a shadow and nothing more.

I began to feel a real presence in that house and for the longest time after, I felt very connected to it. It was not until that night, however, that I felt that there might be something there that did not want us to be there.

While the MTGC group was down in the basement filming the interviews for the documentary, I decided to go in and shoot some pictures into the dark of the central museum where the artifacts were kept. I was completely alone and I was being very careful to not touch doors or frames, for fear that I would disturb the equipment that was set up. It turned out that the museum room was the only room not set up with any equipment, ironically enough. The large, heavy wooden door that gave entrance to the room was open about halfway and I stepped inside the pitch-black room so that I could get a better shot. I was not expecting anything to happen, as nothing had really happened on any of my excursions. I stepped a little further to the side of the door, the only light coming from another room. I could not see anything and was having trouble adjusting my camera to get it in focus. My head was down and I was trying to make sure all the settings were correct when...BOOM!!!!! The sound was so loud and so forceful that I screamed, almost dropping the camera in my hand. The door behind me had not slammed shut, as I thought it had. It had slammed open. I scrambled out of the room and stood there in panic and disbelief as to what had just happened. Four other members of the team came running in to find me, certain that I had fallen over equipment or knocked something off. I stammered and stuttered, but they remained absolutely calm. It took me several minutes to get myself together enough to go back in and shoot, but by then, there was nothing. I took Leslie with me and went back to the room. We tried to recreate the door slam, but were unable to. I tried to knock it with my arm, but it did not recreate what happened. Whenever I tried to "accidentally" knock the door, it would bounce back and knock several more times. The door that slammed on me only hit once, as if an imaginary hand had kept it there. To be honest,

This is the door that slammed open on me. Notice how big and heavy it is.

Slave quarters as seen from the back porch of Octagon Hall.

that was about enough proof for me and the night was only beginning at that point.

After that incident, I went outside to catch my breath and to take some pictures of the grounds. The summer kitchen was directly behind the house and that would be used in hot weather so that it would not heat up the rest of the house. There was also a "whistling walkway" from the summer kitchen to the house. When the slaves were bringing in food from the kitchen, they were required to whistle so that the people inside would know that they were not stealing food off the plates. Off to the side of the summer kitchen and behind the main house stands a slave quarters. It is surrounded by fields and trees. There are no lights. As I was standing on the back porch, shooting pictures out into the dark, open field I noticed a large orb at the base of the quarters on one of the pictures. A few seconds later, I took a picture that I have absolutely no explanation for. It

Same building later that night. Notice the large orb outside of the house. There are smaller orbs around it as well.

appears that there is an illuminated figure in the trees. However, the figure is only from the waist up. Upon closer examination, I saw that there was a hand that was clearly visible. I do not know what it was holding; perhaps it was just the memory of holding a rake or a hoe. What is for certain is that I checked with all the other members and all were present and accounted for. No one was outside or near the field behind the slave quarters. Again, this is one more example of the camera capturing something that I know for a fact was not visible to the naked eye.

Conclusion

What still lurks in Octagon Hall? Is it the presence of the family, moving through their everyday actions just like they did in life or is it the Confederate soldiers, wounded and dying in the home itself? Do fear, hate, love, sadness, and joy remain long after the bodies have been put into the ground and begin to decay? There seems to be two options for Octagon Hall. The presences there

I almost threw this picture out without even looking at it. If it had not been for Leslie pointing out that there was something illuminated in the trees, I would not have even seen what was there. What I can tell for certain is that when I zoomed in on this figure, a hand is clearly visible and it's carrying something that is thrown over the shoulder of the figure. Is this Henry coming in from the fields?

could be *residual* elements that linger still, like an image one sees after the lights are off. The other option is that the presences there are *intelligent*, sensing light, dark, cold, warmth, and the presence of others. If this is the case, then the EVPs caught by the MTGC and the owners could be attempting to contact people who come into the house. One can only guess and fabricate meaning from personal experiences or images caught on film. Whatever the case, one thing cannot be denied: *whatever still lingers is active, moving, and does interact with people, whether to startle, frighten, or just play with them*. While Octagon Hall might not be the most haunted place in Kentucky, it is undeniably, in my mind, the most active of any of the places I had been privileged to see. If you're in Kentucky and want a really neat trip out to the country, pull off the expressway and take a walk around the house and grounds of Octagon Hall. You might be surprised, like I was, at what you find.

The Grey Lady of Liberty Hall

Walking the grounds of Liberty Hall, located in our state's capital, Frankfort, I could imagine just for a moment what life would have been like. The grounds and gardens are beautiful and are just a short walk from the lovely Georgian mansion built by one of Kentucky's first Senators, John Brown. Do not be confused as to which John Brown once lived here. This is not the same John Brown who led a raid at Harper's Ferry and was later hanged for his involvement. That particular John Brown still lies "a moldin' in the grave," as the song named for him states. The John Brown that constructed Liberty Hall was no relation to the other Brown and played a major role in the history of Kentucky and the early political situation of the state. His story is, as most of the stories of the early pioneers are, filled with some joy and some sadness. Retrospectively glancing at the stories of the early days, I cannot help but think how little things change through the centuries. Though the days were difficult and the times different, people have pretty much remained the same. Those who came centuries before us still loved, lived, and died just as we do today. Parents still lose children, although not as frequently due to modern medicine. Today we worry about losing children to tragic accidents involving technologies that were not present in the olden days. However, the fact remains that loss still exists and people continue to mourn for those who are lost. It's on that note that the story of Liberty Hall and her inhabitants begins to unfold.

The Brown Family

Frankfort was adopted as our state's capital in 1792, but the land on which it sits was bare and, at the time, led into the Kentucky wilderness. As the land began to open up and people moved to establish their own homes and farms, it was not uncommon to find this land being given to well-established gentlemen and their families. In 1786 James Wilkinson asked the governor of Virginia and famed Revolutionary War hero Patrick Henry to grant him land on which he could build. Patrick Henry gave him the land and Wilkinson began to lay out the city, one of whose primary streets still bears his name. He sold the property where Liberty Hall now sits to a Mr. Andrew Holmes, who then sold it to Kentucky's first US Senator, John Brown. John Brown began construction of the Federal style home in 1796, but it was not completed until 1803 when the windows were finally installed.

John Brown was born in Virginia in 1757. His academic career was an illustrious one, attending the institution now known as Princeton and then later continuing his studies at the prestigious William and Mary College. He read law and actually worked in the law offices of Thomas Jefferson while living in Virginia. John Brown was on his way politically and it was no surprise to anyone that he began his own law practice and established himself as the Virginia delegate of the Kentucky district to the First Continental Congress. At his death, he was the only surviving member of the first Continental Congress. He became Kentucky's first Senator and more than that, became the beloved husband of Margaretta Mason. He was in his forties and she was only twenty-six when they married. However, unlike the marriages of political convenience that ran rampant among the prominent families of the day, theirs was truly a love match, as is evidenced by the remaining letters that were written between the two.

Margaretta moved to Kentucky from her home in New York City and, though distance separated her from her husband on many occasions, her devotion to him and their children – and vice versa – was obvious from the tone of the letters they wrote to each other. The letters focused on many household situations and the education of their children. The tone, the terms of endearment used, and the length indicated a real longing they had for each other. Kentucky Educations Television (KET) did a very nice documentary on the letters between the two, weaving a tale of true love and the experiences of one woman in the pioneer days of Kentucky. During the course of their marriage, they had two sons who survived infancy and childhood, growing into fine men who would carry on the name of one of the most successful and oldest families in the state. Mason, named for Margaretta's family, and Orlando would be the only surviving children. Two other boys died in infancy and then there was the tragic story of their daughter, Euphemia.

The Gray Lady

Mrs. Margaret Varick lived in New York during the time that Margaretta and John were having children and raising their family. It was not uncommon at this time in history for children to fall ill and die of common ailment for which one could take a simple over-the-counter medicine today. In the late 1700s till the early part of the nineteenth century, typhoid, cholera, diphtheria, and many other germy culprits could rob families of all their children and some of the adults — in one fell swoop. People would often drink from common wells using common cups. Water supplies would be tainted with animal waste or other ungodly bacteria and people would consume it without hesitation, not knowing that the underlying cause of all the illnesses could be prevented by a few simple steps and the boiling of water. Then, there were some ailments such as "bilious colic" (which doctors would later re-name appendicitis) that were mislabeled and misunderstood by the doctors of the age. Unfortunately, the "cure" for many of the ailments was worse than the sickness itself. Bleeding to let out the "bad blood" or whatever was infecting the patient often caused sickness or death. Leeches were commonly used to treat maladies from PMS or the vapors, to cancer. The dark ages of medicine were truly not a time one would want to be sick. Unfortunately, the illness and untimely death of the only little girl in the house would become an example of the remedy being worse than the sickness.

There is little information that I could find about what exactly was wrong with Euphemia Helm Brown. Born in 1807, she was the only daughter the couple would ever have. Little is known about her except that it was her sickness and death that brought her Great Aunt Margaret Varick all the way down from New York to do one of two things: help out during the illness of the child, or comfort the grieving family after the child's death. What is known is that when Euphemia took ill in 1814, she was given a medicine called Calomel. Calomel was given as a remedy for intestinal or stomach problems and was used to treat symptoms such as constipation, bowel difficulties, and would also serve as an emetic due to its ability to make those who took it regurgitate whatever was bothering their stomachs. What was not known at the time was that the medication, recognized today by the name Mercuric Chloride, was a very strong poison. Those who took the white, sweet tasting medicine in large doses were actually killed by mercury poisoning, which is a terrible way to die (as if there are really any good ones). This is exactly what happened to Euphemia Brown. Given the medication to help make her better, she actually died from the treatment. The house must have been in absolute chaos and distress at the loss of the only little girl, and it is during this time that Mrs. Varick made her trip. There are stories—and I do not know if they are true or apocryphal—that Mrs. Varick had a heart condition. Upon her arrival at Liberty Hall, she did not have much time to comfort the family. The stress of the death and the long trip from New York took their toll on her and she expired from a heart attack after only being in the home three days. She died in an upstairs bedroom and, some say, lingers there today. Two deaths occurring back-to-back... the deaths of the Brown's two infant sons... medicine that was supposed to help a child live becomes the invisible hand of the Grim Reaper... yes, Liberty Hall has no shortage of sad stories to tell its listener. The historical information is that the two surviving sons would live on and Mason would inherit the property known as Liberty Hall. John Brown, not wanting to see his other son left out completely, built another home just a feet away from Liberty Hall and gave it to his son Orlando. These two homes continue to be of interest for the thrill seeking ghost chaser as well as those who long to savor the stories and architecture of the past.

Short, sad, and sweet... That is how I would characterize the next possible candidate for the haunting of Liberty Hall. At the turn of the nineteenth century, balls were often held in honor of those who were artists or performers. Liberty Hall and the ever gracious Browns were no stranger to this kind of entertaining. A very beautiful and talented Spanish opera singer had stopped in Frankfort to give a performance and was invited to the Brown's home for a late supper party. During the course of the evening, she walked out to view the gardens and possibly stroll down along the edge of the Kentucky River, which was not far away. The gardens, which are lovely and beckon one to amble among the shrubs and flowers planted there, were inviting, but would not have led to the boundaries of other homes, as they do today. In that time, it would have still been framed by dense forest and woodland. The singer, whose name I could not find anywhere, left the home and was never seen again. She simply disappeared. Could she have slipped by the edge of the river and drowned? Quite possibly. However, the river was dragged and no body ever turned up in any of the searches. Could she have been walking by herself and been abducted by a band of wild men? Certainly. There were criminals even then. Another possible explanation is that natives who inhabited the area could have abducted her. For all anyone really knows, aliens could have abducted her. The only thing we really know for certain is that she was never seen again.

The Haunting

Unlike other sites mentioned in this book, whatever haunts Liberty Hall is not malevolent or spiteful, according to accounts given by those who have witnessed them. People have reported seeing a small, frail lady, dressed in a gray housedress walking the stairs of Liberty Hall or lingering in the room in which Mrs. Varick died. The descriptions given of her all coincide with her actual historical description, so it is very likely her. It has been said that she is a caring soul who will tuck the covers in around visitors or watch over them as they sleep. People have also reported the more frightening apparition of a beautiful young woman who runs through the garden outside, her mouth open as if screaming for help. This has been accepted as the ghost of the young opera singer, presumably running for help or her life. Some reports have also included a young man who looks into the window from the outside. Rumor has it that there was a young man who, during the War of 1812, fell in love with a young lady living in the house. Unable to gain the affection of the family, he was never able to marry the lady inside. He continues to pine after her, even in the afterworld. As a historian, I take this story with a grain of salt, since I know that the only daughter died at a young age and that the dates do not correspond with that of the Brown family. It is, however, a good story and I do not discount the fact that some disembodied spirit might still be hovering outside, begging admittance.

It was unfortunate that when I went to shoot pictures at this location, the entire home was being renovated. I could only get pictures from the outside, which yielded nothing unusual. I was reluctant to shoot the windows, which are still original to the home. They have an unusual texture to them, giving off an almost oily appearance, and I did not want to compromise any pictures that might have captured someone looking out. The gardens, where numerous figures have been spotted, gave up nothing on the particular day that I was there. Had it not been for a kindly worker who gave me permission to come onto the property, I might not have been able to get the shots that I did. Whatever I did not find on this trip does not mean that this building is not paranormally active. By all accounts, this is a very active spot and I am wondering how the renovations will affect the activity in the house once it is completed.

Cave Hill Cemetery

The History

I have always been skeptical that a cemetery would hold any kind of paranormal activity, since the people who repose there died elsewhere. The last resting place of a person would not be the familiar territory that they knew in life, nor would it hold any kind of sentimental value for a spirit who was longing to return to what it knew in life. I have been surprised at how wrong I have been about many things, including the paranormal world, during the course of writing this book. Therefore, when Cave Hill turned up on my list of possible places to investigate, I had to take a second look. After all, the Old Pioneer Cemetery in Bardstown yielded a number of interesting photographs that I would have never looked twice at before writing this book. In the spirit of curiosity and personal interest in the graves of the many historic people who are buried there, I decided one Sunday afternoon to go and have a look.

If you have never had the opportunity to visit Cave Hill, you probably have never spent much time in Louisville. It is a beautifully kept cemetery that houses a lovely duck pond. As a child, my parents, like many parents of my contemporaries, thought that getting us darling little ducklings for Easter was a brilliant idea. There would be dozens of children all along the streets of Louisville out caring for their ducklings in the back yards of their homes, their parents smiling fondly at what a precious photo op this was for them. We would get them little pools to waddle about in and we would feed them

Little girls as they might have been in life.

out of our hands. Unfortunately, the backyards in Louisville are not that large, and ducks, like children, continue to grow. After awhile, it became obvious to the parents that the ducks could not stay in the backyard forever. If the neighbor's dogs didn't get to them first, many times possums and raccoons would. So, every summer you could see the parade of parents coming, ducks in hand, to the large lake in Cave Hill Cemetery. There, the ducks would be free to come and go as they pleased and the children would be able to go visit them whenever they wished. It was a win-win situation. I like to think that now, even as I gaze upon the duck pond and the children throwing bread to them, that they are feeding the grand-ducklings and great grand ducklings of the parents we let go there so many years ago. It was as I thought about this that the realization came to me that this is exactly the purpose of a place like Cave Hill. People come here year after year, generation to generation, to find their place in the grand scheme of the world. Almost everyone whose family has been in Kentucky for fifty years or more probably has some tie to someone buried there. By visiting the site where someone is buried, there is forged a real connection to the past, which is not abstract. Underneath the dirt is buried someone who is related to you. Did they have your eyes or hair like yours? What about the birthmark or the crook in the nose? Whatever the commonality, one certainty remains. Whoever lies there was once as alive as the person standing above. Coming face to face with our own mortality is precisely the reason that Cave Hill began. And, like the ducks, those of us who

Precious little girl on bended knee.

Tranquil green lady turns her face heavenward.

visit there know that even when we are gone, in some small way we have left our mark on the world around us.

When William Johnston's family first laid the bricks for their home and farm in Louisville, they had no idea that the land they called home would become one of the most beloved spots in Louisville. After the Johnston's sold the property, their house was converted into what was known as a "Pest House." It was used as a place where people who needed to be quarantined, due to their infection with a communicable disease, were kept in isolation from the rest of the populace. It would later be used as a maternity hospital and a home for inebriates. While not the most pleasant of places at the time, no one knew that the Victorian fascination with death and the rituals surrounding it would take hold in this place, creating a spectacular cemetery and garden spot for the final repose of the soul. To understand the beauty of such a place as Cave Hill, one must understand the Victorian mind set about death. The Victorians were obsessed with death. Due in part to the fact that death was all around them, one scholar on the subject, Carol Christ, explained that the Victorians developed rituals to help them deal with it. Her studies suggest that the average life span for a person in Victorian England was forty-four years of age. Fifty-five percent of all children born would not live past age five. Death was a common part of home life and people had to find ways to live with the parting of those who they loved. There were special garments that must be worn by widows, even down to the black ribbons on their undergarments. Queen Victoria herself set the precedent by making sure that everything remained just as her beloved Albert left it — right down to the glass that he drank his last dose of medicine from. It remained the same and untouched for the forty years that she mourned him. In America, things were much the same. People developed ways to deal with the loss, as loss was a common occurrence. Those who were sick did not have the luxury of a sterile hospital room where one could expire and then be quickly whisked away to a morgue. People were born at home, lingered at home, and then died there. In no way could the family remove themselves from the sight, the smell, or

Three children from the same family.

the reality of the finality of the human condition. They learned to deal with staring death straight in the face by creating deathbed and mourning rituals, which for the most part, modern people must do without. Death has become something that we distance ourselves from, removing our loved ones to places outside the home for their wakes and burials. Nineteenth century people did not have that luxury. Writer D. Lyn Hunter had this to say about the subject, "From our modern point of view, it is easy to make fun of these rituals, but Christ said Victorian culture recognized death as an integral part of life and they maintained an honest understanding of loss and grief. Modern society has a tendency to deal with death in more medical terms. 'We don't die any differently now than back then,' said Christ. 'But how death is represented has changed drastically.'"(12)

So what does all this background on how the Victorians dealt with death have to do with Cave Hill Cemetery, you might ask? In addition to being just really interesting information, it hopefully gives a little insight as to why a place of such grief and mourning became one of the most beautiful spots in Louisville. It was during this time that people began to look for ways to cope with death in a more positive way. Instead

Infant asleep in a shell.

of throwing the bodies of diseased transients and indigents into sink holes and backyard plots, the planners of the city had the foresight to plan a place that would be beautiful and natural, becoming almost a metaphor for the passing away experience. The writers of the Cave Hill website put it eloquently when they stated that:

> Death was not to be abhorred and feared. It was full of promise, hope, and rejuvenation; and the sorrow associated with it was accompanied by joy and revelation. Death was merely a transition, and as such, a natural setting for burials became desirable. Asleep in nature elicited a much different feeling than being confined and neglected in shabby plots and yards that many times themselves spread diseases and compounded the problem. Their only saving grace was as sources of cadavers for medical schools.[13]

The grounds would eventually become the repository for many famous local people. Colonel Harland Sanders of Kentucky Fried Chicken fame would rest there next to the extremely well rendered bust that was sculpted by his daughter in 1973. Gideon Shyrock, who built Liberty Hall and many other famous landmarks in Kentucky, is also buried there along with the Kentucky Giant, Big

Jim Porter. The list of famous people is well worth a look, as some of the most famous buildings in Kentucky have their namesakes laid to rest there. So the question remains, who haunts this locale?

Glowing Tombstones

The stories abound that people have seen strange lights and glowing tombstones in this peaceful, tranquil place. There have been pictures taken where people will swear that they see faces in doors and orbs all around. I stopped to ask one of the guards who worked at Cave Hill if he could tell me anything about any strange happenings. He replied that quite honestly, he had heard the stories, but had seen nothing himself. Cave Hill Cemetery turns up on many lists of haunted places and that cannot be denied. There have been investigations done and Cave Hill still comes up as a place that is actively haunted. Perhaps it takes the right person on the right day at the right time to tempt spirit activity, but on the day I went, I could find nothing on any of my pictures to corroborate these stories. Of course, that does not mean much, but in the spirit of honest reporting, I cannot say that anything wanted to show itself to me.

Blooming azaleas surround a memorial in Cave Hill Cemetery.

Conclusion

So you might be asking yourself, has the skeptical writer been convinced after all the pictures and all the stories? After all the door slamming, disembodied voices, floating orbs, and apparitions, I must say that I lean more toward belief these days than disbelief. As with most situations in this life, just when we are convinced that we have everything under control and figured out, something strolls along to make us question why we ever thought we knew it all in the first place. It is the same with spirits. I am reminded of what one gentleman I spoke with said. When asked what it would take for him to believe in ghosts, he replied that it would take a 20-30 second conversation where he asked questions and the spirit replied in an intelligent, coherent way. He said that if, and when, this ever occurs, he will put away his equipment, monitors, and probably quit the ghost chasing business forever. At that point, he would be finished and the questions in his mind would be answered. While that thought is interesting, I am not sure that I would stop at that point. It might just be the beginning of an entirely new search and perhaps, for now, some questions are better left unanswered. As for me, I will admit that I will never again look at pictures the same way. I will never hear a story the same way and I surely will never poo-poo the far fetched recounts of doors that slam on their own and misty figures that walk and then disappear. Experience may not answer all questions, but it certainly does add a new dimension to the reasons we ask them in the first place.

Instead of skirting the issue, you probably want to know if I believe now or not. Let's just say, I'll let you know when I get finished researching and writing about the Ghosts of Lexington!

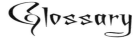Glossary

Afterlife: This term is commonly referred to as what happens to a person after death. Many cultures, both ancient and modern believe that when the body dies, there is an immortal part of the self that lives on in some form.

Anomaly: Something that cannot be explained logically or has a reasonable explanation. An anomaly could be anything from a mist to a mysterious light that shows up with no reasonable explanation of why it is there.

Apparition: While I am hesitant to use the word "ghost," the word apparition applies to any vapor-like mist that appears to take the form of a person. Traditionally, this is what people think of when they hear the word "ghost."

Entity: This term applies to beings who are both living and dead.

EMF: EMF is short for Electro Magnetic Frequency. This device detects levels of energy and is used in investigations to detect "hot" or "active" spots where ghosts may be. When high energy levels are detected, the machine emits a high pitched beeping noise and the investigator must look closely to determine whether the device is detecting a ghostly presence or just a fuse box or microwave oven. The EMF meter does not distinguish between the two, so it is imperative that the investigator use the utmost integrity and rule out any other option.

EVP: EVP is short for Electronic Voice Phenomena and is usually a hand held device that records voices of the living and the dead. Used by professional investigators, this will capture voices that the regular ear cannot detect.

Ghost: This term is extremely ambiguous, as many people define it many ways. Commonly, it is used to explain the lingering presence of a person after he or she has passed away. One explanation that is also interesting is that a ghost is the presence of a person who has not "crossed over" or gone into a final resting place. Some speculate that the ghost may be attached to particular places or people, but should not be confused with a "Spirit."

Haunted: Referring to a setting or specific place where ghosts, spirits, or poltergeists are found. Both people and locations may be "haunted."

Orb: A round area that is translucent or transparent in nature. Found in photography, the camera will capture what the eye cannot see. Many believe that orbs are a spirit presence. Note: There are many explanations for orbs. Dust, water droplets, or condensation in the air may appear as an "orb," so it's extremely difficult to say for certain whether these are spirits or a natural occurrence at the location. It's necessary to take many comparative shots to see if the same orbs appear time and time in a location.

Paranormal: Coming from the Greek meaning "around," the paranormal skirts around the edges of what we know as "normal" everyday life. The paranormal lies outside the realm of the natural world as we know it.

Poltergeist: Coming from the German meaning "noisy ghost" as poltergeist is not a benign entity, but often mischievous and destructive in nature. While a ghost or a spirit may haunt a location, their interactions with people are not usually negative. With a poltergeist, the interaction is almost always negative in nature, such as in the breaking of dishes, moving of furniture, clanking, and /or crashing sounds.

Residual Energy: Many researchers believe that the spirit portion of a person's being is essentially energy. Upon death, many believe that the person's energy leaves a sort of "footprint" on the area that it knew during life. Residual Energy is not the same thing as a "ghost" because it is more of an after image of the person or being upon a specific area. The main difference between a ghost and residual energy appears to be intelligence. Residual Energy repeats paths and patterns, as if constantly being rewound and played over again. Ghosts may respond to external stimulation such as someone speaking to them, asking them to do something, or simply acting on their own.

Spirit: Not to be confused with a ghost, a spirit is often used synonymously with the word "soul." Some believe that the spirit may linger in a place even after it has "crossed over."

Bibliography and Works Cited

1. Florida Historical Society. *Makers of America: An Historical and Biographical Work by an Able Corps*. A.B. Caldwell, Florida, 1909. Original from the New York Public Library, volume 2. Digitized November 11, 2005.
   (http://books.google.com/books?id=yDo6VhLx6fEC&pg=PA321&lpg=PA321&dq=%22major+thomas+h+hays%22&source=web&ots=YGQoOlxS4b&sig=LTFLwUwgloDAEgV51F8lykOCoFc#PPA321,M1)

2. *New York Times* Archive. Dedicated at Chickamauga; The Granite Monument Erected by the State of Kentucky. May 4, 1899.
   (http://query.nytimes.com/gst/abstract.html?res=9900EEDF1430E132A25757C0A9639C94689ED7CF)

3. http://www.dodgejeffgen.com/archive/Consumption.htm

4. Yoffe, Emily. "What's Consumption and Why Did it Kill Nicole Kidman?" Slate. Posted Tuesday, June 5, 2001. http://www.slate.com/id/1007801/

5. National Institute of Allergy and Infectious Disease. "I Must Die." http://www3.niaid.nih.gov/topics/tuberculosis/Research/researchFeatures/history/historical_die.htm

6. http://supersearch.mudcat.org/@displaysong.cfm?SongID=4632

7. DeMechelle, Matthew and Potter, Gary. "Sin City Revisited: A Case Study of the Official Sanctioning of Organized Crime in an "Open City." Justice and Police Studies, Eastern Kentucky University. http://www.rootsweb.com/~kycampbe/newportgambling.htm

8. http://archiver.rootsweb.com/th/read/KYHARDIN/2006-05/1146935535

9. http://home.hiwaay.net/~woliver/Litt_Laws_Vol3.html

10. http://www.daytonhistorybooks.citymax.com/page/page/3509157.htm

11. Dorsey, Dr. G. Volney. Washington Township and the City of Piqua. http://troydailynews.com/genealogy/stories/hist1880/wash-twp.htm. Computerized Heritage Association, 1999.

12. Hunter, D. Lyn. "A Victorian Obsession with Death: Fetishistic Rituals Helped Survivors Cope with the Loss of Loved Ones." Posted April 5, 2000. http://berkeley.edu/news/berkeleyan/2000/04/05/death.html

13. "Early History." Cave Hill Cemetery Website. http://www.cavehillcemetery.com/earlyhistory.html

This statue of a woman mourning her husband can be found in Cave Hill Cemetery.